Fodor's New Pocket Puerto Rico

Reprinted from *Fodor's Caribbean*

Fodor's Travel Publications, Inc.
New York • Toronto • London • Sydney • Auckland
http://www.fodors.com/

Fodor's Pocket Puerto Rico

Editors: Caroline V. Haberfeld, Jennifer Paull
Contributors: Robert Blake, Judy Blumenberg, Janet Foley, Pete Hamill, Jonathan Runge, Heidi Sarna, Helayne Schiff, Mary Ellen Schultz, M. T. Schwartzman
Creative Director: Fabrizio La Rocca
Associate Art Director: Guido Caroti
Photo Researcher: Jolie Novak
Cartographer: David Lindroth
Cover Photograph: Martin/Uniphoto
Text Design: Between the Covers

Copyright

Special Sales

Fodor's Travel Publications are available at special discounts for bulk purchases for sales promotions or premiums. Special editions, including personalized covers, excerpts of existing guides, and corporate imprints, can be created in large quantities for special needs. For more information, contact your local bookseller or write to Special Markets, Fodor's Travel Publications, 201 East 50th Street, New York, NY 10022. Inquiries from Canada should be directed to your local Canadian bookseller or sent to Random House of Canada, Ltd., Marketing Department, 1265 Aerowood Drive, Mississauga, Ontario L4W 1B9. Inquiries from the United Kingdom should be sent to Fodor's Travel Publications, 20 Vauxhall Bridge Road, London SW1V 2SA, England.

PRINTED IN THE UNITED STATES OF AMERICA

10 9 8 7 6 5 4 3 2 1

CONTENTS

Maps

ON THE ROAD WITH FODOR'S

WE'RE ALWAYS thrilled to get letters from readers, especially one like this:

It took us an hour to decide what book to buy and we now know we picked the best one. Your book was wonderful, easy to follow, very accurate, and good on pointing out eating places, informal as well as formal. When we saw other people using your book, we would look at each other and smile.

Our editors and writers are deeply committed to making every Fodor's guide "the best one"— not only accurate but always charming, brimming with sound recommendations and solid ideas, right on the mark in describing restaurants and hotels, and full of fascinating facts that make you view what you've traveled to see in a rich new light.

On the Web

Also check out Fodor's Web site (http://www.fodors.com/), where you'll find travel information on major destinations around the world and an ever-changing array of travel-savvy interactive features.

New and Noteworthy

With the expansion of airline service in the Caribbean, **American Airlines** now routes an increasing number of flights through San Juan on its subsidiary, American Eagle. Old San Juan is getting its own enhancement: the **Horned Dorset Primavera** plans to establish a second boutique hotel in one of the area's historic houses. In addition, the newly renovated **Gran Hotel El Convento** and the **Wyndham Old San Juan Hotel and Casino** are scheduled to open in late 1996.

How to Use This Book

Organization

Chapter 1 is **Essential Information.** Its first section, **Important Contacts,** gives addresses and telephone numbers of organizations and companies that offer destination-related services and detailed information and publications. **Smart Travel Tips,** the second section, gives specific information on how to accomplish what you need to in Puerto Rico as well as tips on savvy traveling. Both sections are in alphabetical order by topic.

Icons and Symbols

★   Our special recommendations

✗   Restaurant

🏨   Lodging establishment

✗🏨   Lodging establishment whose restaurant warrants a detour

🦆   Good for kids (rubber duckie)

☞   Sends you to another section of the guide for more information

✉   Address

☎   Telephone number

🕐   Opening and closing times

💰   Admission prices (those we give apply only to adults; substantially reduced fees are almost always available for children, students, and senior citizens)

Hotel Facilities

We always list the facilities that are available—but we don't specify whether they cost extra: When pricing accommodations, always ask what's included.

Assume that hotels operate on the **European Plan** (EP, with no meals) unless we note that they use the **Full American Plan** (FAP, with all meals), the **Modified American Plan** (MAP, with breakfast and dinner daily), the **Continental Plan** (CP, with a Continental breakfast daily), or are **all-inclusive** (all meals and most activities).

Restaurant Reservations and Dress Codes

Reservations are always a good idea; we note only when they're essential or when they are not accepted. Book as far ahead as you can, and reconfirm when you get to town. Unless otherwise noted, the restaurants listed are open daily for lunch and dinner. We mention dress only when men are required to wear a jacket or a jacket and tie.

Credit Cards

The following abbreviations are used: **AE**, American Express; **D**, Discover; **DC**, Diners Club; **MC**, MasterCard; and **V**, Visa.

Don't Forget to Write

You can use this book in the confidence that all prices and opening times are based on information supplied to us at press time; Fodor's cannot accept responsibility for any errors. Time inevitably brings changes, so always confirm information when it matters—especially if you're making a detour to visit a specific place. In addition, when making reservations be sure to mention if you have a disability or are traveling with children, if you prefer a private bath or a certain type of bed, or if you have specific dietary needs or any other concerns.

Were the restaurants we recommended as described? Did our hotel picks exceed your expectations? Did you find a museum we recommended a waste of time? If you have complaints, we'll look into them and revise our entries when the facts warrant it. If you've discovered a special place that we haven't included, we'll pass the information along to our correspondents and have them check it out. So send your feedback, positive *and* negative, to the Puerto Rico editor at 201 East 50th Street, New York, New York 10022—and have a wonderful trip!

Karen Cure
Editorial Director

DESTINATION: PUERTO RICO

PUERTO RICO IS SO complex in its history and culture—so rich in the variety of its activities and attractions—that it would be a great mistake to think of this lovely island as simply another resort area. It is of course a wonderful playground—its beaches are sandy and properly palm fringed; its casinos, discos, and nightclubs quicken pulses; its hotels and *paradores* cater to both the jaded jet setter and the incurable romantic; and its restaurants pay homage to the cuisines of the world.

The decision that faces all visitors to Puerto Rico is what *type* of visit to have. The choices are numerous: a beach vacation in San Juan's fashionable Condado or Isla Verde areas; a stay in Old San Juan, whose narrow colonial streets and historic sites are easily explored on foot; a drive-around-the-island adventure, stopping in other Puerto Rican cities like Ponce and Mayagüez, a visit to a self-contained resort like Dorado Beach, Cerromar Beach, or Palmas del Mar; or a drive to a *parador* like Gripiñas, a former 19th-century coffee plantation in the hills above Ponce. Those who want to get away from it all can even hop a plane to one of Puerto Rico's off-shore islands—Culebra or Vieques, for example.

First-time visitors will probably elect to stay in San Juan—in either the old or beachfront sections— and take day trips to various attractions like Luquillo Beach, El Yunque rain forest, Ponce ("The Pearl of the South"), Mayagüez on the western coast, and Arecibo Observatory and the Rio Camuey Cave Park in the northwestern section of the island.

Because of Puerto Rico's benevolent climate, the island is a popular vacation spot throughout the year. Nevertheless, the crowds tend to come during the late fall to early spring period, escaping the winter weather up north. Puerto Rico attracts a wide variety of visitors: vacationers and honeymooners on package plans, cruise passengers docking at San Juan's handsome old port, sun-seeking Canadians and vacationing college students, the rich and famous checking into luxury resorts like Dorado and Cerromar Beach, and sports lovers flying (or sailing) in for the golf, tennis, fishing, swimming, surfing, scuba diving, and horse racing. Although the sun, the sea and the casinos are perhaps the biggest initial draws, most visitors leave with rave reviews for the warm and friendly people, the relaxed atmosphere throughout the island, the compelling history and culture, and the fascinating shops, galleries, and restaurants.

— J.P. MacBean

x

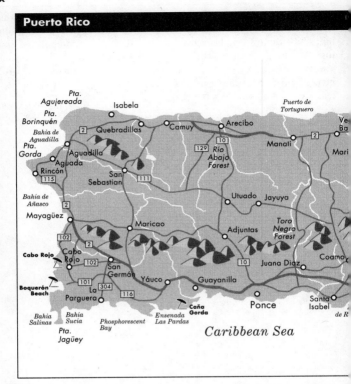

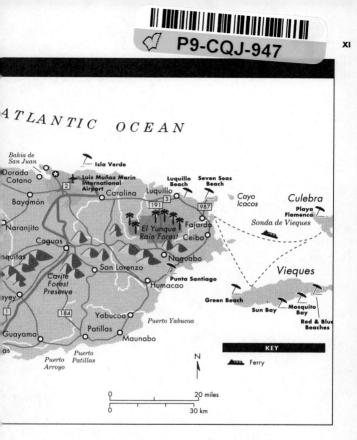

ATLANTIC OCEAN

Bahia de San Juan
Dorado
Catano
Isla Verde
Luis Muñoz Marin International Airport
Carolina
Luquillo
Luquillo Beach
Seven Seas Beach
Cayo Icacos
Culebra
Playa Flamenco
Sonda de Vieques
Bayamón
Naranjito
El Yunque Rain Forest
Fajardo
Ceiba
Caguas
nquitas
San Lorenzo
Naguabo
Vieques
Carite Forest Preserve
Humacao
Punta Santiago
yey
Green Beach
Sun Bay
Mosquito Bay
Red & Blue Beaches
Guayama
Yabucoa
Patillas
Puerto Yabucoa
Guayama
Maunabo
Puerto Arroyo
Puerto Patillas

KEY
Ferry

N

0   20 miles
0   30 km

The Caribbean

THE BAHAMAS

Turks
and
Caicos
Islands

Cuba

Dominican
Republic

Haiti

Hispaniola

GREATER

Port-au-
Prince

Santo
Domingo

ANT

N

Caribbean

0   200 miles
0   300 km

Aruba

Willemstad

Curaço

VENEZUELA

COLOMBIA   Maracaibo

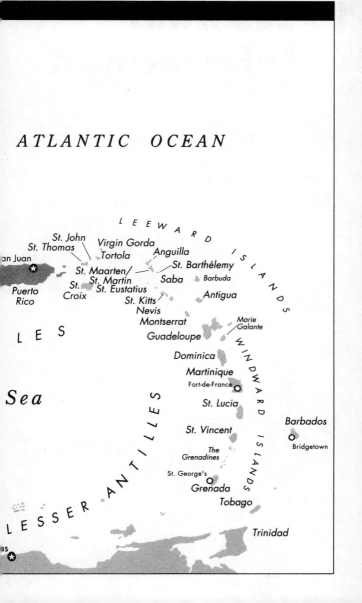

ATLANTIC OCEAN

LEEWARD ISLANDS

St. John
St. Thomas
Virgin Gorda
Tortola
Anguilla
St. Barthélemy
an Juan
St. Maarten/
St. Martin
Saba
Barbuda
Puerto
Rico
St.
Croix
St. Eustatius
St. Kitts
Antigua
Nevis
Montserrat
Marie
Galante
Guadeloupe
WINDWARD ISLANDS
Dominica
Martinique
Fort-de-France
LES
Sea
St. Lucia
Barbados
St. Vincent
Bridgetown
The
Grenadines
St. George's
Grenada
Tobago
LESSER ANTILLES
Trinidad

1 Essential Information

IMPORTANT CONTACTS

An Alphabetical Listing of Publications, Organizations, and Companies That Will Help You Before, During, and After Your Trip

AIR TRAVEL

The **Luis Muñoz Marín International Airport** (☎ 787/462–3147), east of downtown San Juan, is one of the easiest and cheapest destinations to reach in the Caribbean.

CARRIERS

The Luis Muñoz Marín International Airport is the Caribbean hub for **American Airlines** (☎ 800/433–7300). Other carriers with nonstop service include **American Trans Air (ATA)** (☎ 800/382–5892); **Continental** (☎ 800/231–0856); **Delta** (☎ 800/221–1212); **Midway** (☎ 800/446–4392); **Northwest** (☎ 800/447–4747); **Tower Air** (☎ 800/452–5531); **TWA** (☎ 800/892–4141); **United** (☎ 800/241–6522); and **USAir** (☎ 800/428–4322). Puerto Rico–based **Carnival Airlines** (☎ 800/437–2110) operates daily nonstop flights from New York, Newark, Miami, and Orlando to Ponce and Aguadilla as well as San Juan.

Foreign carriers include **Air France** (☎ 800/237–2747); **British Airways** (☎ 800/247–9297); **BWIA** (☎ 800/327–7401); **Iberia** (☎ 800/772–4642); **LACSA** (☎ 800/225–2272); and **Lufthansa** (☎ 800/645–3880).

CAR RENTAL

All major U.S. car-rental agencies are represented on the island, including **Avis** (☎ 787/721–4499 or 800/331–1212), **Hertz** (☎ 787/791–0840 or 800/654–3131), **Budget** (☎ 787/791–3685 or 800/472–3325), and **National** (☎ 787/791–1805 or 800/328–4567). Local rental companies, sometimes less expensive, include **Caribbean Rental** (☎ 787/724–3980), **Charlie Car Rental** (☎ 787/728–2418 or 800/289–1227), and **L & M Car Rental** (☎ 787/725–8416).

CRUISING

To find out which ships are sailing where and when they depart, contact the **Caribbean Tourism Organization** (⊠ 20 E. 46th St., 4th floor, New York, NY 10017, ☎ 212/682–0435).

Cruise lines that make stops in Puerto Rico include **Carnival Cruise Lines** (⊠ Carnival Pl., 3655 N.W. 87th Ave., Miami, FL 33178, ☎ 305/599–2600); **Celebrity Cruises** (⊠ 5200 Blue

Lagoon Dr., Miami, FL 33126, ☎ 800/437–3111); **Club Med** (✉ 40 W. 57th St., New York, NY 10019, ☎ 800/258–2633); **Costa Cruise Lines** (✉ World Trade Center, 80 S.W. 8th St., Miami, FL 33130, ☎ 800/462–6782); **Crystal Cruises** (✉ 2121 Ave. of the Stars, Los Angeles, CA 90067, ☎ 800/446–6620); **Cunard Line** (✉ 555 5th Ave., New York, NY 10017, ☎ 800/221–4770); **Diamond Cruise Inc.** (✉ 600 Corporate Dr., Suite 410, Fort Lauderdale, FL 33334, ☎ 800/333–3333); **Dolphin/Majesty Cruise Lines** (✉ 901 South American Way, Miami, FL 33132, ☎ 800/532–7788); **Holland America Line** (✉ 300 Elliott Ave. W, Seattle, WA 98119, ☎ 800/426–0327); **Norwegian Cruise Line** (✉ 95 Merrick Way, Coral Gables, FL 33134, ☎ 800/327–7030); **Princess Cruises** (✉ 10100 Santa Monica Blvd., Los Angeles, CA 90067, ☎ 310/553–1770); **Royal Caribbean Cruise Line** (✉ 1050 Caribbean Way, Miami, FL 33132, ☎ 800/327–6700); and **Seabourn Cruise Line** (✉ 55 Francisco St., San Francisco, CA 94133, ☎ 800/351–9595).

CUSTOMS

CANADIANS

Contact **Revenue Canada** (✉ 2265 St. Laurent Blvd. S, Ottawa, Ontario K1G 4K3, ☎ 613/993–0534) for a copy of the free brochure **"I Declare/Je Déclare"** and for details on duty-free limits.

For recorded information (within Canada only), call 800/461–9999.

U.K. CITIZENS

HM Customs and Excise (✉ Dorset House, Stamford St., London SE1 9NG, ☎ 0171/202–4227) can answer questions about U.K. customs regulations and publishes a free pamphlet, **"A Guide for Travellers,"** detailing standard procedures and import rules.

DISABILITIES AND ACCESSIBILITY

ORGANIZATIONS

TRAVELERS WITH HEARING IMPAIRMENTS➤ Contact the **American Academy of Otolaryngology** (✉ 1 Prince St., Alexandria, VA 22314, ☎ 703/836–4444, FAX 703/683–5100, TTY 703/519–1585).

TRAVELERS WITH MOBILITY PROBLEMS➤ Contact the **Information Center for Individuals with Disabilities** (✉ Box 256, Boston, MA 02117, ☎ 617/450–9888 or 800/462–5015 in MA; TTY 617/424–6855); **Mobility International USA** (✉ Box 10767, Eugene, OR 97440, ☎ and TTY 541/343–1284, FAX 541/343–6812), the U.S. branch of a Belgium-based organization with affiliates in 30 countries; **MossRehab Hospital Travel Information Service** (☎ 215/456–9600, TTY 215/456–9602), a telephone information resource for travelers with physical disabilities; the **Society for the Advancement of Travel for the Handi-**

capped (⌧ 347 5th Ave., Suite 610, New York, NY 10016, ☎ 212/447–7284, FAX 212/725–8253; membership $45); and **Travelin' Talk** (⌧ Box 3534, Clarksville, TN 37043, ☎ 615/552–6670, FAX 615/552–1182) which provides local contacts worldwide for travelers with disabilities.

TRAVELERS WITH VISION IMPAIRMENTS➤ Contact the **American Council of the Blind** (⌧ 1155 15th St. NW, Suite 720, Washington, DC 20005, ☎ 202/467–5081, FAX 202/467–5085) for a list of travelers' resources or the **American Foundation for the Blind** (⌧ 11 Penn Plaza, Suite 300, New York, NY 10001, ☎ 212/502–7600 or 800/232–5463, TTY 212/502–7662).

DIVING

For a list of training facilities where you can earn your diving certification card, write to **PADI** (⌧ Professional Association of Diving Instructors, 1251 E. Dyer Rd., #100, Santa Ana, CA 92705).

EMERGENCIES

Police, fire, and medical emergencies: ☎ 911. **Hospitals:** Hospitals in the Condado/Santurce area with 24-hour emergency rooms are **Ashford Community Hospital** (⌧ 1451 Av. Ashford, ☎ 787/721–2160) and **San Juan Health Centre** (⌧ 200 Av. De Diego, ☎ 787/725–0202). **Pharmacies:** In San Juan, **Walgreens** (⌧ 1130 Av. Ashford, Condado, ☎ 787/725–1510) operates a 24-hour pharmacy; in Old San Juan, try **Puerto Rico Drug Company** (⌧ 157 Calle San Francisco, ☎ 787/725–2202). Walgreens operates more than 30 pharmacies on the island.

GAY AND LESBIAN TRAVEL

ORGANIZATIONS

The **International Gay Travel Association** (⌧ Box 4974, Key West, FL 33041, ☎ 800/448–8550, FAX 305/296–6633), a consortium of more than 1,000 travel companies, can supply names of gay-friendly travel agents, tour operators, and accommodations.

PUBLICATIONS

The premier international travel magazine for gays and lesbians is *Our World* (⌧ 1104 N. Nova Rd., Suite 251, Daytona Beach, FL 32117, ☎ 904/441–5367, FAX 904/441–5604; $35 for 10 issues). The 16-page monthly *"Out & About"* (☎ 212/645–6922 or 800/929–2268, FAX 800/929–2215; $49 for 10 issues and quarterly calendar) covers gay-friendly resorts, hotels, cruise lines, and airlines.

LODGING

APARTMENT AND VILLA RENTAL

Among the companies to contact are **At Home Abroad** (⌧ 405 E. 56th St., Suite 6H, New York, NY 10022, ☎ 212/421–9165, FAX 212/752–1591); **Europa-Let** (⌧ 92 N. Main St., Ashland, OR 97520, ☎ 541/482–5806 or 800/462–

4486, FAX 541/482–0660); **Property Rentals International** (⊠ 1008 Mansfield Crossing Rd., Richmond, VA 23236, ☎ 804/378–6054 or 800/220–3332, FAX 804/379–2073); **Rental Directories International** (⊠ 2044 Rittenhouse Sq., Philadelphia, PA 19103, ☎ 215/985–4001, FAX 215/985–0323); **Rent-a-Home International** (⊠ 7200 34th Ave. NW, Seattle, WA 98117, ☎ 206/789–9377 or 800/488–7368, FAX 206/789–9379); **Unusual Villas & Island Rentals** (⊠ 101 Tempsford La., Penthouse 9, Richmond, VA 23226, ☎ 804/288–2823 or 800/768–0280, FAX 804/288–2823); **Vacation Home Rentals Worldwide** (⊠ 235 Kensington Ave., Norwood, NJ 07648, ☎ 201/767–9393 or 800/633–3284, FAX 201/767–5510); **Villas and Apartments Abroad** (⊠ 420 Madison Ave., Suite 1003, New York, NY 10017, ☎ 212/759–1025 or 800/433–3020, FAX 212/755–8316); and **Villas International** (⊠ 605 Market St., Suite 510, San Francisco, CA 94105, ☎ 415/281–0910 or 800/221–2260, FAX 415/281–0919). Members of the travel club **Hideaways International** (⊠ 767 Islington St., Portsmouth, NH 03801, ☎ 603/430–4433 or 800/843–4433, FAX 603/430–4444; $99 per yr) receive two annual guides plus quarterly newsletters and arrange rentals among themselves.

MONEY

ATMS

For specific **Cirrus** locations, call 800/424–7787; for **Plus** locations, consult the Plus directory at your local bank.

CURRENCY EXCHANGE

If your bank doesn't exchange currency, contact **Thomas Cook Currency Services** (☎ 800/287–7362 for locations). **Ruesch International** (☎ 800/424–2923 for locations) can also provide you with foreign banknotes before you leave home and publishes a number of useful brochures, including a "Foreign Currency Guide" and "Foreign Exchange Tips."

WIRING FUNDS

Funds can be wired via **MoneyGram^{SM}** (for locations and information in the U.S. and Canada, ☎ 800/926–9400) or **Western Union** (for agent locations or to send money using MasterCard or Visa, ☎ 800/325–6000; in Canada, 800/321–2923; in the U.K., 0800/833833; or visit the Western Union office at the nearest major post office).

PASSPORTS AND VISAS

CANADIANS

For fees, documentation requirements, and other information, call the Ministry of Foreign Affairs and International Trade's **Passport Office** (☎ 819/994–3500 or 800/567–6868).

U.K. CITIZENS

For fees, documentation requirements, and to request an emergency passport, call the **London
Passport Office** (☎ 0990/210410).

SIGHTSEEING

Old San Juan can be seen either
on a self-guided walking tour or
on the free trolley. To explore the
rest of the city and the island, consider renting a car. (We do, however, recommend a guided tour of
the vast El Yunque rain forest.) If
you'd rather not do your own
driving, there are several tour
companies you can call. Most San
Juan hotels have a tour desk that
can make arrangements for you.
The three standard half-day tours
(at $15–$30) are of Old and New
San Juan; Old San Juan and the
Bacardi Rum Plant; and Luquillo
Beach and El Yunque rain forest.
All-day tours ($25–$45) can include a trip to Ponce, a day at El
Comandante Racetrack, or a combined tour of the city and El
Yunque rain forest.

Leading tour operators include
Gray Line of Puerto Rico (☎ 787/
727–8080); **Normandie Tours, Inc.**
(☎ 787/722–6308); **Rico Suntours**
(☎ 787/722–2080 or 787/722–
6090); **Tropix Wellness Tours**
(☎ 787/268–2173); and **United
Tour Guides** (☎ 787/725–7605
or 787/723–5578). **Cordero
Caribbean Tours** (☎ 787/786–
9114 or 787/780–2442 evenings)
runs tours in air-conditioned
limousines for an hourly rate.

TELEPHONES

The area code for Puerto Rico
changed from 809 to 787 as of
March 1, 1996.

For local access numbers abroad,
contact **AT&T** USADirect (☎ 800/
874–4000), **MCI** Call USA (☎
800/444–4444), or **Sprint** Express
(☎ 800/793–1153).

TOUR OPERATORS

PACKAGES

For independent vacation packages throughout the Caribbean,
including Puerto Rico, contact
Adventure Vacations (✉ 10612
Beaver Dam Rd., Hunt Valley,
MD 21030-2205, ☎ 410/785–
3500 or 800/638–9040, FAX 410/
584–2771); **American Airlines Fly
AAway Vacations** (☎ 800/321–
2121); **Certified Vacations** (✉ Box
1525, Fort Lauderdale, FL 33302,
☎ 954/522–1440 or 800/233–
7260); **Delta Dream Vacations**
(☎ 800/872–7786); **Globetrotters**
(✉ 139 Main St., Cambridge, MA
02142, ☎ 617/621–9911 or
800/333–1234); **USAir Vacations**
(☎ 800/455–0123); or **United Vacations** (☎ 800/328–6877). **Funjet
Vacations,** based in Milwaukee,
Wisconsin, and **Gogo Tours,** based
in Ramsey, New Jersey, sell packages only through travel agents.
Club Med (✉ 40 W. 57th St., New
York, NY 10019, ☎ 800/258–
2633) sells cruises and packages
that include charter air at its family, couples, and singles resorts
throughout the Caribbean.

Regional operators specialize in putting together packages for travelers from their local area. Arrangements may include charter or scheduled air. Contact **Apple Vacations** (⌂ 25 N.W. Point Blvd., Elk Grove Village, IL 60007, ☎ 708/640–1150 or 800/365–2775); **Friendly Holidays** (⌂ 1983 Marcus Ave., Lake Success, NY 11042, ☎ 800/344–5687); **GWV International** (⌂ 300 1st Ave., Needham, MA 02194-2721, ☎ 617/449–5450 or 800/225–5498); **Trans National Travel** (⌂ 2 Charlesgate W, Boston, MA 02215, ☎ 617/262–0123 or 800/262–0123, FAX 617/638–3310); and **Travel Impressions** (⌂ 465 Smith St., Farmingdale, NY 11735, ☎ 516/845–8000 or 800/284–0044, FAX 516/845–8095).

THEME TRIPS

GOLF➤ Packages including accommodations, confirmed tee times, and golfing fees and lessons are offered by **Stine's Golftrips** (⌂ Box 2314, Winter Haven, FL 33883-2314, ☎ 813/324–1300 or 800/428–1940, FAX 941/325–0384).

HEALTH➤ **Spa-Finders** (⌂ 91 5th Ave., #301, New York, NY 10003-3039, ☎ 212/924–6800 or 800/255–7727) represents spas on many Caribbean islands.

SCUBA DIVING➤ **Rothschild Dive Safaris** (⌂ 900 West End Ave., #1B, New York, NY 10025-3525, ☎ 212/662–4858 or 800/359–0747, FAX 212/749–6172) has diving trips throughout the Caribbean.

VILLA RENTALS➤ Contact **Unusual Villas & Island Rentals** (⌂ 101 Tempsford La., Penthouse 9, Richmond, VA 23226, ☎ FAX 804/288–2823) or **Villas International** (⌂ 605 Market St., San Francisco, CA 94105, ☎ 415/281–0910 or 800/221–2260, FAX 415/281–0919).

TRAVEL AGENCIES

For names of reputable agencies in your area, contact the **American Society of Travel Agents** (⌂ ASTA, 1101 King St., Suite 200, Alexandria, VA 22314, ☎ 703/739–2782), the **Association of Canadian Travel Agents** (⌂ 1729 Bank St., Suite 201, Ottawa, Ontario K1V 7Z5, ☎ 613/521–0474, FAX 613/521–0805), or the **Association of British Travel Agents** (⌂ 55-57 Newman St., London W1P 4AH, ☎ 0171/637–2444, FAX 0171/637–0713).

VISITOR INFORMATION

Before you go, contact the **Puerto Rico Tourism Company** (⌂ Box 6334, San Juan, PR 00914, ☎ 787/721–2400). From the States, you can call toll-free at ☎ 800/223–6530. Other branches: ⌂ *575 5th Ave., 23rd floor, New York, NY 10017,* ☎ *212/599–6262,* FAX *212/818–1866;* ⌂ *3575 W. Cahuenga Blvd., Suite 560, Los Angeles, CA*

90068, ☎ 213/874–5991, FAX
213/874–7257; ⊠ 901 Ponce de
León Blvd., Suite 604, Coral
Gables, FL 33134, ☎ 305/445–
9112, FAX 305/445–9450. In the
United Kingdom, contact the
tourism office: ⊠ 11a W. Halkin
St., London SW1X 8JL, ☎ 0171/
333–0333.

On Puerto Rico, the government-
sponsored **Puerto Rico Tourism
Company** (⊠ Paseo la Princesa,
Old San Juan, Puerto Rico 00902,
☎ 787/721–2400) is an excellent
source for maps and printed
tourist materials. Be sure to pick
up a free copy of ¿Qué Pasa?, the
official visitors' guide.

Information offices are also found
at **Luis Muñoz Marín International
Airport** in Isla Verde (☎ 787/791–
1014 or 787/791–2551) and **La**

Casita (☎ 787/722–1709), near
Pier 1 in Old San Juan. Out on
the island, information offices are
located in **Ponce** (⊠ Fox Delicias
Mall, 2nd floor, Plaza Las
Delicias, ☎ 787/840–5695),
Aguadilla (⊠ Rafael Hernández
Airport, ☎ 787/890–3315),
Cabo Rojo (⊠ Rte. 100, Km 13.7,
☎ 787/851–7070), and in many
towns' city halls on the main
plaza. Offices are usually open
weekdays from 8 to noon and 1
to 4:30.

WEATHER
For current conditions and fore-
casts, plus the local time and helpful travel tips, call the **Weather
Channel Connection** (☎ 900/932–
8437; 95¢ per minute) from a
Touch-Tone phone.

SMART TRAVEL TIPS

Basic Information on Traveling in Puerto Rico and Savvy Tips to Make Your Trip a Breeze

AIR TRAVEL

If time is an issue, **always look for nonstop flights,** which require no change of plane. If possible, **avoid connecting flights,** which stop at least once and can involve a change of plane, even though the flight number remains the same; if the first leg is late, the second waits.

For better service, **fly smaller or regional carriers,** which often have higher passenger satisfaction ratings. Sometimes they have such in-flight amenities as leather seats or greater legroom and they often have better food.

FROM THE AIRPORT

Taxi Turisticos (☞ Taxis, *below*) charge set rates depending on the destination. Uniformed and badged officials help you find a cab at the airport and provide written information about fares. To Isla Verde, the fare is $8; to Condado, it's $12; to Old San Juan, it's $16. If you don't hail one of these cabs, you're at the mercy of the meter and the cabdriver.

BUSES

The **Metropolitan Bus Authority (AMA)** (☎ 787/250–6064) oper-ates *guaguas* (buses) that thread through San Juan. The fare is 25¢, and the buses run in exclu-sive lanes, *against the traffic* on major thoroughfares, stopping at magenta, orange, and white signs marked *Parada* or *Parada de Guaguas.* The main terminals are Covadunga parking lot and Plaza de Colón, in Old San Juan, and Capetillo Terminal in Rio Piedras, next to the central busi-ness district.

CAR RENTALS

U.S. driver's licenses are valid in Puerto Rico for three months. If you plan to drive across the is-land, arm yourself with a good map and be aware that there are many unmarked roads up in the mountains. Many service stations in the central mountains do not take credit cards. Speed limits are posted in miles, distances in kilo-meters, and gas prices in liters.

Prices start at about $30 (plus in-surance), with unlimited mileage. Discounts are offered for long-term rentals, and insurance can be waived for those who rent with American Express or gold credit cards (be sure to check with your credit-card company before renting). Some discounts are offered for AAA or 72-hour advance bookings. Most car rentals have shuttle service to or from the airport and the pickup point.

Roads in Puerto Rico are generally well marked; however, a good road map is helpful when traveling to more remote areas on the island. Some car-rental agencies distribute free maps of the island when you pick up your car. These maps lack detail and are usually out-of-date due to new construction. The simplest thing to do is head to the nearest gas station—most of them sell better maps. Good maps are also available at the **Book Store** (⊠ 257 Calle San José, Old San Juan, ☎ 787/724–1815).

CRUISES

Cruising the Caribbean is perhaps the most relaxed and convenient way to tour this beautiful part of the world: You get all of the amenities of a Stateside hotel and enough activities to guarantee fun, even on rainy days. Cruising through the islands is an entirely different experience from staying on one island.

Cruise ships usually call at several Caribbean ports on a single voyage but are at each port for only one night. Thus, although you may be exposed to several islands, you don't get much of a feel for any one of them.

As a vacation, a cruise offers total peace of mind. All important decisions are made long before boarding. The itinerary is set, and the total cost of your vacation is known almost to the penny. For details, see Fodor's *Worldwide Cruises and Ports of Call 1997*; the Cruise Primer chapter is particularly helpful if you're cruising for the first time.

To get the best deal on a cruise, **consult a cruise-only travel agency.**

CUSTOMS AND DUTIES

To speed your clearance through customs, **keep receipts for all your purchases abroad** and **be ready to show the inspector what you've bought.** If you feel that you've been incorrectly or unfairly charged a duty, you can **appeal assessments in dispute.** First ask to see a supervisor. If you are still unsatisfied, **write to the port director** of your point of entry, sending your customs receipt and any other appropriate documentation. The address will be listed on your receipt. If you still don't get satisfaction, you can take your case to customs headquarters in Washington.

IN CANADA

If you've been out of Canada for at least seven days, you may bring in C$500 worth of goods duty-free. If you've been away for fewer than seven days but for more than 48 hours, the duty-free allowance drops to C$200; if your trip lasts between 24 and 48 hours, the allowance is C$50. You cannot pool allowances with family members. Goods claimed under the C$500 exemption may follow you by mail; those claimed under the lesser exemptions must accompany you.

Alcohol and tobacco products may be included in the seven-day and 48-hour exemptions but not in the 24-hour exemption. If you meet the age requirements of the province or territory through which you reenter Canada, you may bring in, duty-free, 1.14 liters (40 imperial ounces) of wine or liquor *or* 24 12-ounce cans or bottles of beer or ale. If you are 16 or older, you may bring in, duty-free, 200 cigarettes, 50 cigars or cigarillos, and 400 tobacco sticks or 400 grams of manufactured tobacco. Alcohol and tobacco must accompany you on your return.

An unlimited number of gifts with a value of up to C$60 each may be mailed to Canada duty-free. These do not affect your duty-free allowance on your return. Label the package "Unsolicited Gift— Value Under $60." Alcohol and tobacco are excluded.

IN THE U.K.

From countries outside the European Union, including those in the Caribbean, you may import, duty-free, 200 cigarettes, 100 cigarillos, 50 cigars, or 250 grams of tobacco; 1 liter of spirits or 2 liters of fortified or sparkling wine or liqueurs; 2 liters of still table wine; 60 milliliters of perfume; 250 milliliters of toilet water; plus £136 worth of other goods, including gifts and souvenirs.

DISABILITIES AND ACCESSIBILITY

As a rule, very few attractions and sights are equipped with ramps, elevators, or wheelchair-accessible rest rooms. However, major new properties are planning with the needs of travelers with disabilities in mind. Wherever possible in our lodging listings, we indicate whether special facilities are available.

When discussing accessibility with an operator or reservationist, **ask hard questions.** Are there any stairs, inside *or* out? Are there grab bars next to the toilet *and* in the shower/tub? How wide is the doorway to the room? To the bathroom? For the most extensive facilities, meeting the latest legal specifications, **opt for newer accommodations,** which more often have been designed with access in mind. Older properties or ships must usually be retrofitted and may offer more limited facilities as a result. Be sure to **discuss your needs before booking.**

HEALTH

There are few real health hazards. The small lizards you'll see a good deal of are harmless, and poisonous snakes are hard to find.

The worst problem may well be the tiny sand flies known as no-see-ums, which tend to appear after a rain, near wet or swampy ground, and around sunset. You may want to **bring along a good repellent.**

Sunburn or sunstroke can be serious. A long-sleeve shirt, a hat, and long pants or a beach wrap are essential on a boat, for midday at the beach, and whenever you go out sightseeing. **Use sunblock lotion** on nose, ears, and other sensitive areas, **limit your sun time** for the first few days, and be sure to **drink enough liquids.**

DIVERS' ALERT
Scuba divers take note: **Do not fly within 24 hours of scuba diving.**

LANGUAGE

Puerto Rico's official language is Spanish, and although English is widely spoken, you will probably want to take a Spanish phrase book along if you rent a car to travel around the island.

LODGING

Plan ahead and **reserve a room well before you travel to Puerto Rico.** If you have reservations but expect to arrive later than 5 or 6 PM, tell the management in advance. Unless so advised, some places will not hold your reservations after 6 PM. Also, be sure to **find out what the quoted rate includes**—use of sports facilities and equipment, airport transfers, and

the like—and whether the property operates on the European Plan (EP, with no meals), Continental Plan (CP, with Continental breakfast), Breakfast Plan (BP, with full breakfast), Modified American Plan (MAP, with two meals), or Full American Plan (FAP, with three meals), or is All-inclusive (including three meals, all facilities, and drinks unless otherwise noted). Be sure to **bring your deposit receipt** with you in case questions arise.

Decide whether you want a hotel on the leeward side of the island (with calm water, good for snorkeling) or the windward (with waves, good for surfing). Decide, too, whether you want to pay the extra price for a room overlooking the ocean or pool. Also **find out how close the property is to a beach**; at some hotels you can walk barefoot from your room onto the sand; others are across a road or a 10-minute drive away.

Nighttime entertainment is alfresco in Puerto Rico, so if you go to sleep early or are a light sleeper, ask for a room away from the dance floor.

Air-conditioning is not a necessity, but it can be a plus if you enjoy an afternoon snooze. Breezes are best in second-floor rooms, particularly corner rooms. If you like to sleep without air-conditioning, make sure that windows can be opened and have screens.

In this book, we categorize properties by price rather than quality. Prices are intended as a guideline only. Larger hotels with more extensive facilities cost more, but Puerto Rico also has smaller places with charm, individuality, and prices that make up for their lack of activities—which are generally available on a pay-per-use basis everywhere.

APARTMENT AND VILLA RENTAL

If you want a home base that's roomy enough for a family and comes with cooking facilities, **consider taking a furnished rental.** This can also save you money, but not always—some rentals are luxury properties (economical only when your party is large). Home-exchange directories list rentals—often second homes owned by prospective house swappers—and some services search for a house or apartment for you and handle the paperwork. Some send an illustrated catalog; others send photographs only of specific properties, sometimes at a charge; up-front registration fees may apply.

MAIL

Puerto Rico uses U.S. postage stamps and has the same mail rates (22¢ for a postcard, 32¢ for a first-class letter). Post offices in major Puerto Rican cities offer Express Mail next-day service to the U.S. mainland and to Puerto Rican destinations.

MONEY

ATMS

CASH ADVANCES➤ Before leaving home, **make sure that your credit cards have been programmed for ATM use** in the Caribbean. Note that Discover is accepted mostly in the United States. Local bank cards often do not work overseas either; **ask your bank about a Visa debit card,** which works like a bank card but can be used at any ATM displaying a Visa logo.

TRANSACTION FEES➤ Although fees charged for ATM transactions may be higher abroad than at home, Cirrus and Plus exchange rates are excellent, because they are based on wholesale rates offered only by major banks.

CURRENCY

The U.S. dollar is the official currency of Puerto Rico.

TRAVELER'S CHECKS

Whether or not to buy traveler's checks depends on where you are headed; **take cash to rural areas and small towns, traveler's checks to cities.** The most widely recognized checks are issued by American Express, Citicorp, Thomas Cook, and Visa. These are sold by major commercial banks for 1%–3% of the checks' face value—it pays to **shop around.** Both American Express and Thomas Cook issue checks that can be countersigned and used by either you or your traveling companion. So you won't be left with excess foreign currency, **buy a few checks in small denominations** to cash toward the end of your trip. Before leaving home, **contact your issuer for information on where to cash your checks** without incurring a transaction fee. Record the numbers of all your checks, and keep this listing in a separate place, crossing off the numbers of checks you have cashed.

WIRING MONEY

For a fee of 3%–10%, depending on the amount of the transaction, you can have money sent to you from home through Money-Gram[SM] or Western Union (☞ Money *in* Important Contacts *above*). The transferred funds and the service fee can be charged to a MasterCard or Visa account.

PACKING FOR PUERTO RICO

Dress on the islands is light and casual. Bring loose-fitting clothes made of natural fabrics to see you through days of heat and humidity. Take a cover-up for the beaches, not only to protect you from the sun but also to wear to and from your hotel room. Bathing suits and immodest attire are sometimes frowned upon off the beach. A sun hat is advisable, but you don't have to pack one, since inexpensive straw hats are available everywhere. For shopping and sightseeing, bring walking shorts, jeans, T-shirts, long-sleeve cotton shirts, slacks,

and sundresses. You'll need a light sweater for protection from the trade winds, and at higher altitudes. Evenings are casual, but "casual" can range from really informal to casually elegant, depending on the establishment. A tie is rarely required, but jackets are sometimes de rigueur in fancier restaurants and casinos.

Bring an extra pair of eyeglasses or contact lenses in your carry-on luggage, and if you have a health problem, **pack enough medication** to last the trip or have your doctor write you a prescription using the drug's generic name, because brand names vary from country to country (you'll then need a duplicate prescription from a local doctor). It's important that you **don't put prescription drugs or valuables in luggage to be checked,** because it could go astray. To avoid problems with customs officials, carry medications in the original packaging. Also, don't forget the addresses of offices that handle refunds of lost traveler's checks.

PASSPORTS AND VISAS

Puerto Rico is a commonwealth of the United States, and U.S. citizens do not need passports to visit the island. British citizens must have passports. Canadian citizens need proof of citizenship (preferably a passport).

SAFETY

San Juan, like any other big city and major tourist destination, has its share of crime, so guard your wallet or purse on the city streets. Puerto Rico's beaches are open to the public, and muggings can occur at night even on the beaches of the posh Condado and Isla Verde tourist hotels. While you certainly can and should explore the city and its beaches, using common sense will make your stay more secure and enjoyable. Don't leave anything unattended on the beach. Leave your valuables in the hotel safe, and stick to the fenced-in beach areas of your hotel. Always lock your car and stash valuables and luggage out of sight. Avoid deserted beaches at night.

TAXIS

The Puerto Rico Tourism Company has recently instituted a much-needed and well-organized taxi program for tourists. Taxis painted white and sporting the *garita* (sentry box) logo and **Taxi Turístico** label charge set rates depending on the destination; they run from the airport or the cruise-ship piers to Isla Verde, Condado/Ocean Park, and Old San Juan, with rates ranging from $6 to $16. Metered cabs authorized by the **Public Service Commission** (☎ 787/751–5050) start at $1

and charge 10¢ for every additional tenth of a mile, 50¢ for every suitcase, and $1 for home or business calls. Waiting time is 10¢ for each 45 seconds. The minimum charge is $3. Be sure the driver starts the meter. You can also call **Major Taxicabs** (☎ 787/723–2460) in San Juan and **Ponce Taxi** (☎ 787/840–0088).

PÚBLICOS

Públicos (literally, "public cars"), with yellow license plates ending in "P" or "PD," scoot to towns throughout the island, stopping in each town's main plaza. These 17-passenger vans operate primarily during the day, with routes and fares fixed by the Public Service Commission. In San Juan, the main terminals are at the airport and at Plaza Colón on the waterfront in Old San Juan.

TROLLEYS

If your feet fail you in Old San Juan, climb aboard the free open-air trolleys that rumble and roller-coast through the narrow streets. Departures are from La Puntilla and from the marina, but you can board anywhere along the route.

2 Exploring Puerto Rico

FEW CITIES IN THE CARIBBEAN are as steeped in Spanish tradition as Puerto Rico's Old San Juan. Originally built as a fortress enclave, the old city has myriad attractions, including restored 16th-century buildings, museums, art galleries, bookstores, and 200-year-old houses with balustraded balconies of filigreed wrought iron overlooking narrow cobblestone streets. This Spanish tradition also spills over into the island's countryside, from its festivals celebrated in honor of various patron saints in the little towns to the *paradores,* inexpensive but accommodating inns whose concept originated in Spain.

Puerto Rico has hundreds of beaches with every imaginable water sport and acres of golf courses and tennis courts. It has, in San Juan's sophisticated Condado and Isla Verde areas, glittering hotels; flashy, Las Vegas–style shows; casinos; and frenetic discos. It has the ambience of the Old World in the seven-square-block area of the old city and in its quiet colonial towns. Out in the countryside lie its natural attractions, including the extraordinary, 28,000-acre Caribbean National Forest, more familiarly known as the El Yunque rain forest, with 100-foot-high trees (more than 240 species of them) and dramatic mountain ranges. You can hike through forest reserves laced with trails, go spelunking in vast caves, and explore coffee plantations and sugar mills. Having seen every sight on the island, you can then do further exploring on the islands of Culebra, Vieques, Icacos, and Mona, where aquatic activities, such as snorkeling and scuba diving, prevail.

Puerto Rico, 110 miles long and 35 miles wide, was populated by several tribes of Indians when Columbus landed on the island on his second voyage in 1493. In 1508, Juan Ponce de León, the frustrated seeker of the Fountain of Youth, established a settlement on the island and became its first governor, and in 1521, he founded Old San Juan. For three centuries, the French, Dutch, and English tried unsuccessfully to wrest the island from Spain. In 1897, Spain granted the island dominion status. In 1899, as a result of the Spanish American War, Spain ceded the island to the United States, and in 1917, Puerto Ricans became U.S. citizens. In 1952, Puerto Rico became a semiautonomous commonwealth territory of the United States.

If you're a U.S. citizen, you need neither passport nor visa when you land at the bustling Luis Muñoz Marín International Airport, outside San Juan. You don't have to clear customs, and you don't have to explain yourself to an immigration official. English is widely spoken, though the official language is Spanish.

OLD SAN JUAN

Numbers in the margin correspond to points of interest on the Exploring Old San Juan map.

Old San Juan, the original city founded in 1521, contains authentic and carefully preserved examples of 16th- and 17th-century Spanish colonial architecture, some of the best in the New World. More than 400 buildings have been beautifully restored in a continuing effort to preserve the city. Graceful wrought-iron balconies, decorated with lush green hanging plants, extend over narrow streets paved with blue-gray stones (*adequines,* originally used as ballast for Spanish ships). The old city is partially enclosed by the old walls, dating from 1633, that once completely surrounded it. Designated a U.S. National Historic Zone in 1950, Old San Juan is chockablock with shops, open-air cafés, private homes, tree-shaded squares, monuments, plaques, pigeons, and people. The traffic is awful. Get an overview of the inner city on a morning's stroll (bearing in mind that this "stroll" includes some steep climbs). However, if you plan to immerse yourself in history or to shop, you'll need two or three days. You may want to set aside extra time to see El Morro and Fort San Cristóbal, especially if you're an aficionado of military history. UNESCO has designated each fortress a World Heritage Site; each is also a National Historic Site. Both are administered by the National Park Service; you can take one of its tours or wander around on your own.

4

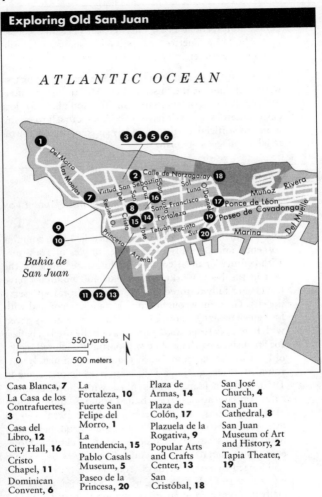

ATLANTIC OCEAN

Bahía de
San Juan

| 0 | 550 yards |
| 0 | 500 meters |

N

Casa Blanca, **7**

La Casa de los
Contrafuertes,
3

Casa del
Libro, **12**

City Hall, **16**

Cristo
Chapel, **11**

Dominican
Convent, **6**

La
Fortaleza, **10**

Fuerte San
Felipe del
Morro, **1**

La
Intendencia, **15**

Pablo Casals
Museum, **5**

Paseo de la
Princesa, **20**

Plaza de
Armas, **14**

Plaza de
Colón, **17**

Plazuela de la
Rogativa, **9**

Popular Arts
and Crafts
Center, **13**

San
Cristóbal, **18**

San José
Church, **4**

San Juan
Cathedral, **8**

San Juan
Museum of Art
and History, **2**

Tapia Theater,
19

Sights to See

7 **Casa Blanca.** The original structure on this site, not far from the ramparts of El Morro, was a frame house built in 1521 as a home for Ponce de León. But Ponce de León died in Cuba, never having lived in it, and it was virtually destroyed by a hurricane in 1523, after which Ponce de León's son-in-law had the present masonry home built. His descendants occupied it for 250 years. From the end of the Spanish-American War in 1898 to 1966, it was the home of the U.S. Army commander in Puerto Rico. A museum devoted to archaeology is on the second floor. The lush surrounding gardens, cooled by spraying fountains, are a tranquil spot for a restorative pause. ⊠ *1 Calle San Sebastián,* ☎ *787/724–4102.* ☞ *$2.* ☉ *Wed.–Sat. 9–noon and 1–4:30.*

3 **La Casa de los Contrafuertes.** This building is also known as the Buttress House because wide exterior buttresses support the wall next to the San Jose Plaza. The house is one of the oldest remaining private residences in Old San Juan. Inside is the Pharmacy Museum, a re-creation of an 18th-century apothecary shop, and the Latin American Graphic Arts Museum and Gallery, which hosts occasional exhibitions. ⊠ *101 Calle San Sebastián, Plaza de San José,* ☎ *787/724–5477.* ☞ *Free.* ☉ *Wed.–Sun. 9–4:30.*

12 **Casa del Libro.** This 18th-century building contains exhibits devoted to books and bookbinding. The museum's 5,000 books include many rare volumes. ⊠ *255 Calle Cristo,* ☎ *787/723–0354.* ☞ *Free.* ☉ *Tues.–Sat. 11–4:30.*

16 **City Hall.** Called the *Alcaldía,* this structure was built between 1604 and 1789. In 1841, extensive renovations were done to make the Alcaldía resemble Madrid's city hall, with arcades, towers, balconies, and a lovely inner courtyard. A tourist information center and an art gallery are on the first floor. ⊠ *North side of Plaza de Armas,* ☎ *787/724–7171, ext. 2391.* ☉ *Weekdays 8–4.*

11 **Cristo Chapel.** According to legend, in 1753 a young horseman, carried away during festivities in honor of the patron saint, raced down the street and plunged over the steep precipice. A witness to the tragedy promised to build a chapel if the young man's life could be saved. Historical records maintain the man died, though legend contends that he lived. Inside is a small silver altar, dedicated to the Christ of Miracles. ⊠ *Calle Cristo.* ⊗ *Tues. 10–3:30 and on most Catholic holidays.*

❻ Dominican Convent. Built by Dominican friars in 1523, the convent often served as a shelter during Carib Indian attacks and, more recently, as headquarters for the Antilles command of the U.S. Army. Now home to the Institute of Puerto Rican Culture, the beautifully restored building contains an ornate 18th-century altar, religious manuscripts, artifacts, and art. The Institute also maintains a bookshop here. The convent is the intended future home of the city's museum of fine arts. Classical concerts are occasionally held here. ⊠ *98 Calle Norzagaray,* ☎ *787/721–6866.* 🖅 *Free.* ⊗ *Mon.–Sat. 9–5.*

❿ La Fortaleza. Sitting on a hill overlooking the harbor, La Fortaleza, the Western Hemisphere's oldest executive mansion in continual use and official residence of the present governor of Puerto Rico, was built as a fortress. The original primitive structure, built in 1540, has seen numerous changes over the past four centuries, resulting in the present collection of marble and mahogany, medieval towers, and stained-glass galleries. Guided tours are conducted every hour on the hour in English, on the half hour in Spanish. ⊠ *Calle Recinto Oeste,* ☎ *787/721–7000, ext. 2211 or 2358.* 🖅 *Free.* ⊗ *Weekdays 9–4.*

❶ Fuerte San Felipe del Morro. Sitting on a rocky promontory on the northwestern tip of the old city is "El Morro," a fortress built by the Spaniards between 1540 and 1783. Rising 140 feet above the sea, the massive six-level fortress covers enough territory to accommodate a nine-hole golf course. It is a labyrinth of dungeons, ramps and barracks, turrets, towers, and tunnels. Built to protect the port, El Morro has a commanding view of the harbor. Its small, air-conditioned museum traces the history of the fortress. Tours and a video show are available in English. ⊠ *Calle Norzagaray,* ☎ *787/729–6960.* 🖅 *Free.* ⊗ *Daily 9–5.*

❶❺ La Intendencia. From 1851 to 1898, this handsome three-story neoclassical building was home to the Spanish Treasury; now it is the headquarters of Puerto Rico's State Department. ⊠ *Calle San José, at the corner of Calle San Francisco,* ☎ *787/722–2121, ext. 230.* ☜ *Free. Tours at 2 and 3 in Spanish, 4 in English.* ⊙ *Weekdays 8–noon and 1– 4:30.*

⑤ Pablo Casals Museum. This museum contains memorabilia of the famed cellist, who made his home in Puerto Rico for the last 16 years of his life. Manuscripts, photographs, and his favorite cellos are on display, in addition to recordings and videotapes of Casals Festival concerts (the latter shown on request). ⊠ *101 Calle San Sebastián, Plaza de San José,* ☎ *787/723–9185.* ☜ *$1.* ⊙ *Tues.–Sat. 9:30–5:30.*

㉑ Paseo de la Princesa. This street down at the port is spruced up with flowers, trees, benches, and street lamps. Take a seat and watch the boats zip across the water.

⑭ Plaza de Armas. This is the original main square of Old San Juan. The plaza, bordered by calles San Francisco, Fortaleza, San José, and Cruz, has a lovely fountain with 19th-century statues representing the four seasons.

NEED A
BREAK?
La Bombonera (⊠ 259 Calle San Francisco, ☎ 787/722– 0658), established in 1903, is known for its strong Puerto Rican coffee and *Mallorca*—a Spanish pastry made of light dough, toasted, buttered, and sprinkled with powdered sugar. Breakfast, for under $5, is served until 11. It's a favorite Sunday-morning gathering place in Old San Juan.

⑰ Plaza de Colón. This bustling square has a statue of Christopher Columbus atop a high pedestal. Originally called St. James Square, it was renamed in honor of Columbus on the 400th anniversary of the discovery of Puerto Rico. Bronze plaques in the base of the statue relate various episodes in the life of the great explorer. On the north side of the plaza is a terminal for buses to and from San Juan. ⊠ *On the pedestrian mall of Calle Fortaleza.*

⑨ Plazuela de la Rogativa. In this little plaza, statues of a bishop and three women commemorate a legend, according to which the British, while laying siege to the city in 1797, mistook the flaming torches of a *rogativa* (religious procession) for Spanish reinforcements and beat a hasty retreat. The monument was donated to the city in 1971 on its 450th anniversary. ⊠ *Caleta de las Monjas.*

🔞 **Popular Arts and Crafts Center.** Run by the Institute of Puerto Rican Culture, the center is located in a colonial building next door to the Casa del Libro (☞ *above*). The center is a superb repository of island craft work, some of which is for sale. ⊠ *253 Calle Cristo,* ☎ *787/722–0621.* 🎟 *Free.* ⊙ *Mon.–Sat. 9–5.*

🔞 **San Cristóbal.** This 18th-century fortress guarded the city from land attacks. Even larger than El Morro, San Cristóbal was known as the Gibraltar of the West Indies. ⊠ *Norzagaray Blvd.,* ☎ *787/729–6960.* 🎟 *Free.* ⊙ *Daily 9–5.*

❹ **San José Church.** With its series of vaulted ceilings, this is a splendid example of 16th-century Spanish Gothic architecture. The church, which is one of the oldest Christian houses of worship in the Western Hemisphere, was built in 1532 under the supervision of the Dominican friars. The body of Ponce de León, the Spanish explorer who came to the New World seeking the Fountain of Youth, was buried here for almost three centuries before being removed in 1913 and placed in the San Juan Cathedral. ⊠ *Calle San Sebastián, Plaza de San José,* ☎ *787/725–7501.* 🎟 *Free.* ⊙ *Mon.–Sat. 8:30–4; mass Sun. at 12:15 PM.*

❽ **San Juan Cathedral.** This great Catholic shrine of Puerto Rico had humble beginnings in the early 1520s as a thatch-topped wood structure. Hurricane winds tore off the thatch and destroyed the church. It was reconstructed in 1540, when the graceful circular staircase and vaulted Gothic ceilings were added, but most of the work on the church was done in the 19th century. The remains of Ponce de León are in a marble tomb near the transept. ⊠ *153 Calle Cristo,* ☎ *787/722–0861.* ⊙ *Weekdays 8:30–4; masses Sat. 7 PM, Sun. 9 AM and 11 AM, weekdays 12:15 PM.*

❷ **San Juan Museum of Art and History.** A bustling marketplace in 1855, this handsome building is now a modern cultural center that houses exhibits of Puerto Rican art. Multi-image audiovisual shows present the history of the island; concerts and other cultural events take place in the huge courtyard. ⊠ *Calle Norzagaray, at the corner of Calle MacArthur,* ☎ *787/724–1875.* 🎟 *Free.* ⊙ *Tues.–Sun. 10–4.*

⑲ **Tapia Theater.** This theater was named after the Puerto Rican playwright Alejandro Tapia y Rivera. Built in 1832 and remodeled in 1949 and again in 1987, the municipal theater is the site of ballets, plays, and operettas. Stop by the box office to find out what's showing. ⌂ *Calle Fortaleza at Plaza de Colón,* ☎ *787/722–0407.*

SAN JUAN

Numbers in the margin correspond to points of interest on the San Juan Exploring map.

You'll need to resort to taxis, buses, públicos, or a rental car to reach the points of interest in "new" San Juan.

Avenida Muñoz Rivera, Avenida Ponce de León, and Avenida Fernández Juncos are the main thoroughfares that cross Puerta de Tierra, just east of Old San Juan, to the business and tourist districts of Santurce, Condado, and Isla Verde. Dos Hermanos Bridge connects Puerta de Tierra with Miramar, Condado, and Isla Grande. Isla Grande Airport, from which you can take short hops, is on the bay side of the bridge. On the other side of the bridge, the Condado Lagoon is bordered by Avenida Ashford, which threads past the high-rise Condado hotels and El Centro Convention Center, and Avenida Baldorioty de Castro Expreso, which barrels all the way east to the airport and beyond. Due south of the lagoon is Miramar, a primarily residential area with fashionable turn-of-the-century homes and a cluster of hotels and restaurants.

South of Santurce is the "Golden Mile"—Hato Rey, the city's bustling financial hub. Isla Verde, with its glittering beachfront hotels, casinos, discos, and public beach, is to the east, near the airport.

Sights to See

㉑ **Capitol.** In Puerta de Tierra is Puerto Rico's Capitol, a white marble building that dates from the 1920s. The grand rotunda, with mosaics and friezes, was completed a few years ago. The seat of the island's bicameral legislature, the Capitol contains Puerto Rico's constitution and is flanked by the

Exploring San Juan

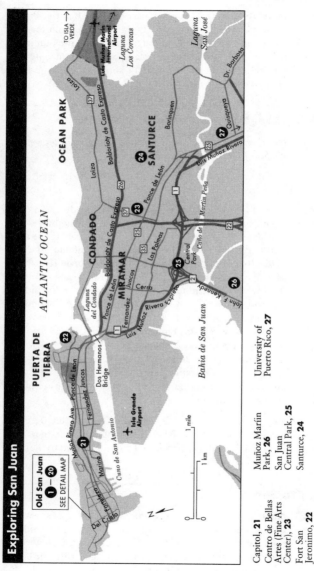

Old San Juan
1 — **20**
SEE DETAIL MAP

TO ISLA VERDE →

Luis Muñoz Marín
International
Airport

Laguna
Los Corozas

Laguna
San José

OCEAN PARK

Dr. Barbosa

Loíza

Baldorioty de Costo Expreso

SANTURCE

Borinquen

Quisqueya

24

Loíza

Ponce de León

Luis Muñoz Rivera

27

ATLANTIC OCEAN

26

37   **23**

Ponce de León

25

Cerro

CONDADO

MIRAMAR

1

Las Palmas

Juncos

35

Caño de Martín Peña

22

Central Park

25

2

26

John F. Kennedy

Laguna
del Condado

Ponce de León

Fernandez

Luis Muñoz Rivera Expreso

PUERTA DE
TIERRA

22

Dos Hermanos
Bridge

Muñoz Rivera Ave.

Fernandez, Juncos

Ponce de León

Marina

Del Cristo

La Fortaleza

21

Caño de San Antonio

Isla Grande
Airport

Bahía de San Juan

N

0   1 km
0   1 mile

Capitol, **21**
Centro de Bellas
Artes (Fine Arts
Center), **23**
Fort San
Jeronimo, **22**

Muñoz Martín
Park, **26**
San Juan
Central Park, **25**
Santurce, **24**

University of
Puerto Rico, **27**

modern buildings of the Senate and the House of Representatives. There are spectacular views from the observation plaza on the sea side of the Capitol. Pick up a booklet about the building from the House Secretariat on the second floor. Guided tours are by appointment only. ⊠ *Av. Ponce de León, Puerta de Tierra,* ☎ *787/721–6040, ext. 2458 or 3548.* 🖾 *Free.* ⊘ *Weekdays 8:30–5.*

㉓ Centro de Bellas Artes. Internationally acclaimed performers appear at the Fine Arts Center. This completely modern facility, the largest of its kind in the Caribbean, has a full schedule of concerts, plays, and operas. ⊠ *Corner of Av. De Diego and Av. Ponce de León, Box 41287, Minillas Station, Santurce 00940,* ☎ *787/725–7353.*

㉒ Fort San Jeronimo. At the eastern tip of Puerta de Tierra, behind the splashy Caribe Hilton, this tiny fort is perched over the Atlantic like an afterthought. Added to San Juan's fortifications in the late 18th century, the structure barely survived the British attack of 1797. Restored in 1983 by the Institute of Puerto Rican Culture, it is now a military museum. At press time, however, the museum remained closed for repairs, and no reopening date had been announced, so visitors could only view the fort from the outside. ⊠ *Calle Rosales, Puerta de Tierra,* ☎ *787/724–5477.*

㉖ Muñoz Marín Park. This idyllic tree-shaded spot is dotted with gardens, lakes, playgrounds, and picnic areas. An aerial gondola connects the park with the parking area and provides a 6½-minute tour of the park. ⊠ *Next to Las Américas Expressway, west on Av. Piñero, Hato Rey,* ☎ *787/751–3353.* 🖾 *Free; parking $1 per vehicle.* ⊘ *Tues.–Sun. 9–5.*

㉕ San Juan Central Park. Southeast of Miramar, Avenida Muñoz Rivera skirts along the northern side of this mangrove-bordered park, a convenient place for jogging and tennis. The park was built for the 1979 Pan-American Games. ⊠ *Cerra St. exit on Rte. 2, Santurce,* ☎ *787/722–1646.* 🖾 *Free.* ⊘ *Mon. 2–9:45, Tues.–Fri. 6:30 AM–9:45 PM, weekends 6:30 AM–6 PM.*

㉔ Santurce. The area that lies between Miramar on the west and the Laguna San José on the east is a busy mixture of shops, markets, and offices. The classically designed **Sacred**

Heart University is the home of the **Museum of Contemporary Puerto Rican Art**, which showcases the works of such modern masters as Rodon, Campeche, and Oller. ⊠ *Barat Bldg.*, ☎ *787/268–0049.* 🖼 *Free.* ☉ *Weekdays 9–5.*

Pescadería Atlántica (⊠ 81 Calle Loiza, ☎ 787/726–6654) is a combination seafood restaurant and retail store. Stop in for a cool drink at the bar and a side dish of *calamares*, lightly breaded squid in a hot, spicy sauce.

㉗ University of Puerto Rico. Río Piedras, a southern suburb of San Juan, is home to the University, located between Avenida Ponce de León and Avenida Barbosa. The university's campus is one of two sites for performances of the Puerto Rico Symphony Orchestra. Theatrical productions and other concerts are also scheduled here throughout the year. The **University Museum** has permanent archaeological and historical exhibits and occasionally mounts special art displays. ⊠ *Next to university's main entrance on Av. Ponce de León, Río Piedras*, ☎ *787/764–0000, ext. 2452.* ☉ *Mon.–Wed. and Fri. 9–4:30, Thurs. 9–9, Sat. 9–3.*

The university's main attraction is the **Botanical Garden**, a lush forest of more than 200 species of tropical and subtropical vegetation. Footpaths lead to a graceful lotus lagoon, a bamboo promenade, an orchid garden, and a palm garden. ⊠ *Intersection of Rtes. 1 and 847 at entrance to Barrio Venezuela, Río Piedras*, ☎ *787/763–4408.* 🖼 *Free.* ☉ *Daily 9–4.*

SAN JUAN ENVIRONS

Numbers in the margin correspond to points of interest on the Exploring Puerto Rico map.

Sights to See

㉚ Bacardi Rum Plant. Visitors can take a 45-minute tour of the bottling plant, museum, and distillery, which has the capacity to produce 100,000 gallons of rum a day. There is a gift shop. (Yes, you'll be offered a sample.) ⊠ *Rte. 888, Km 2.6, Cataño*, ☎ *787/788–1500.* 🖼 *Free.* ☉ *Tours every 20 min Mon.–Sat. 9–10:30 and noon–4.*

㉙ **Barrilito Rum Plant.** On the grounds are a 200-year-old plantation home and a 150-year-old windmill, which is listed in the National Register of Historic Places. ⊠ *Rte. 5.*

㉛ **Bayamón.** In the central park, across from Bayamón's city hall, there are some historical buildings and a 1934 sugarcane train that runs through the park (☎ 787/798–8191), which is open daily 8 AM–5 PM. On the plaza, in the city's historic district, stands the 18th-century Catholic church of Santa Cruz and the old neoclassical city hall, which now houses the **Francisco Oller Art and History Museum.** ⊠ *Calle Santiago Veve,* ☎ *787/787–8620.* ☜ *Free.* ⊙ *Tues.–Sat. 9–4.*

㉘ **Caparra Ruins.** In 1508, Ponce de León established the island's first settlement here. The ruins are that of an ancient fort. Its small **Museum of the Conquest and Colonization of Puerto Rico** contains historical documents, exhibits, and excavated artifacts. (You can see the museum's contents in less time than it takes to say the name.) ⊠ *Rte. 2, Km 6.6, Guaynabo,* ☎ *787/781–4795.* ☜ *Free.* ⊙ *Tues.–Sat. 8:30–4:30.*

OUT ON THE ISLAND

Puerto Rico's 3,500 square miles is a lot of land to explore. While you can get from town to town via público, we don't recommend traveling that way unless your Spanish is good and you know exactly where you're going. The public cars stop in each town's main square, leaving you on your own to reach the beaches, restaurants, paradores, and sightseeing attractions. You'll do much better if you rent a car. Most of the island's roads are excellent. However, there is a tangled web of roads through the mountains, and they are not always well marked. It helps to buy a good road map.

Eastern Puerto Rico

 ㉞ **Las Cabezas de San Juan Nature Reserve.** Opened in 1991, the reserve contains mangrove swamps, coral reefs, beaches, and a dry forest—all of Puerto Rico's natural habitats rolled into a microcosmic 316 acres. Nineteenth-century El Faro, one of the island's oldest lighthouses, is restored and still functioning; its first floor contains a small nature center that has an aquarium and other exhibits. The reserve is open, by reservation only, to the general public Friday–Sunday and to tour groups Wednesday and Thursday. Tours are given on request (in advance, by telephone) four times a day. ⊠ *Rte. 987, Km 5.8,* ☎ *787/722–5882; weekends, 787/860–2560.* ⛝ *$5.*

☾ ❸❷ **Caribbean National Forest.** To take full advantage of the 28,000-acre El Yunque (as it's commonly known) rain forest, go with a tour. Dozens of trails lead through the thick jungle (it sheltered the Carib Indians for 200 years), and the tour guides take you to the best observation points, bathing spots, and waterfalls. Some of the trails are slippery, and there are occasional washouts.

However, if you'd like to drive there yourself, take Route 3 east from San Juan and turn right (south) on Route 191, about 25 miles from the city. The **Sierra Palm Visitor Center** (☎ 787/887–2875) is on Route 191, Km 11.6. Nature talks and programs at the center are in Spanish and English and by appointment only—another good reason to go with a tour group. The center is open daily 9–5 (until 4 in winter).

El Yunque, named after the good Indian spirit Yuquiyu, is in the Luquillo mountain range. The rain forest is verdant with feathery ferns, thick ropelike vines, white tuberoses and ginger, miniature orchids, and some 240 different species of trees. More than 100 billion gallons of rainwater fall on it annually. Rain-battered, wind-ravaged dwarf vegetation clings to the top peaks. (El Toro, the highest peak in the forest, is 3,532 feet.) El Yunque is also a bird sanctuary and the base of the rare Puerto Rican parrot. Millions of tiny, inch-long coquis (tree frogs) can be heard singing (or squawking, depending on your sensibilities). ⊠ *For further information write Caribbean National Forest, Box B, Palmer, PR 00721 or call Catalina Field Office,* ☎ *787/887–2875 or 787/766–5335.*

❸❻ **Culebra.** This island off the east coast of Puerto Rico has lovely white-sand beaches, coral reefs, and a wildlife refuge. In the sleepy town of Dewey, on Culebra's southwestern side, check at the visitor information center at city hall (☎ 787/742–3291) about boat, bike, or car rentals. Don't miss **Playa Flamenco,** 3 miles north of Dewey, or **Playa Soni** on the eastern end of the island: They are two of the prettiest beaches in the Caribbean.

㉟ Fajardo. This is a major fishing and sailing center with thousands of boats tied and stacked in tiers at its three large marinas. Boats can be rented or chartered here, and the *East Wind,* a 53-foot catamaran, can take you out for a full day of snorkeling, swimming, and sunning for $55 per person. Fajardo is also the embarkation point for ferries to the islands of Culebra (a $2.25 fare) and Vieques ($2). ⊠ *Rte. 3.*

㉝ Luquillo Beach. One of the island's best and most popular beaches, Luquillo was once a flourishing coconut plantation. Coral reefs protect its calm, pristine lagoon, making it an ideal place for a swim. The entrance fee is $1 per car, and there are lockers, showers, and changing rooms, as well as stands selling savory Puerto Rican delicacies. The beach gets crowded on weekends, when it seems as if the whole world heads for Luquillo. ⊠ *Rte. 3, Km 35.4.* ▧ *$1 per car.*

㊲ Vieques. On this island off the east coast of Puerto Rico, is **Sun Bay public beach,** a gorgeous stretch of sand with picnic facilities and shade trees. **Red** and **Blue** beaches, located on the U.S. Marine/Camp Garcia base (open to the public 6 AM–6 PM), are superb for snorkeling and privacy. **Mosquito Bay** is best experienced on moonless nights, thanks to the millions of bioluminescent organisms that glow when disturbed—it's like swimming in a cloud of fireflies. Seventy percent of Vieques is owned by the U.S. Navy, ensuring it will remain unspoiled. The deserted beaches—Green, Red, Blue, Navia, and Media Luna—are among the Caribbean's loveliest; you might see a wild *paso fino* horse galloping in the surf. The **visitor information center** (☎ 787/741–5000) is in the fishing village of Esperanza. Both Vieques and Culebra (☞ *above*), parched in contrast to the lush eastern end of Puerto Rico, are havens for colorful "expatriates" escaping the rat race stateside. This is pure old-time Caribbean: fun, funky, and unspoiled—the kind of getaway that is fast disappearing.

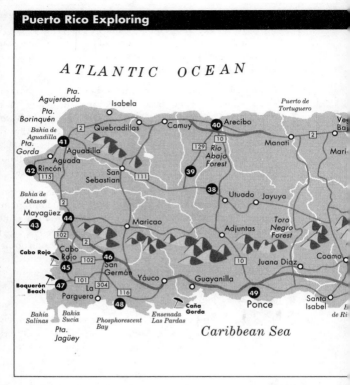

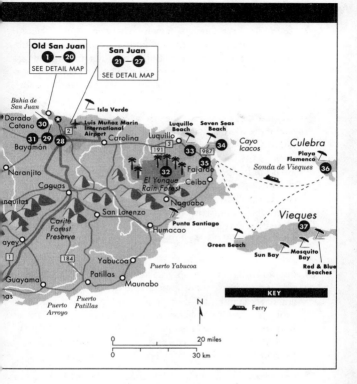

Old San Juan
1 — **20**
SEE DETAIL MAP

San Juan
21 — **27**
SEE DETAIL MAP

Bahia de San Juan

Dorado
Catano **30**

31 **29** **28**

Bayamón

Isla Verde

Luis Muñoz Marin International Airport

Carolina

Luquillo Beach

Luquillo

33

Seven Seas Beach

34

Cayo Icacos

Culebra

Playa Flamenco **36**

Sonda de Vieques

Naranjito

Caguas

El Yunque Rain Forest

32

Fajardo

Ceiba

35

nquitas

San Lorenzo

Naguabo

Vieques

37

Carite Forest Preserve

Humacao

Punta Santiago

ayey

184

Yabucoa

Puerto Yabucoa

Green Beach

Sun Bay

Mosquito Bay

Red & Blue Beaches

1

Patillas

Guayama

Maunabo

N

as

Puerto Arroyo

Puerto Patillas

KEY

Ferry

0   20 miles
0   30 km

Western Puerto Rico

㊶ Aguadilla. In this area, somewhere between Aguadilla and Añasco, south of Rincón, Columbus dropped anchor on his second voyage in 1493. Both Aguadilla and **Aguada,** a few miles to the south, claim to be the spot where his foot first hit ground, and both towns have plaques to commemorate the occasion. ⊠ *Rte. 111.*

㊵ Arecibo Observatory. The town of Arecibo is home to one of the world's largest radar/radio telescopes. A 20-acre radar dish, with a 600-ton suspended platform hovering over it, sits in a 565-foot-deep sinkhole (karst fields, an alien landscape of collapsed limestone sinkholes, are the prevalent geology throughout this part of the island). You can take a self-guided tour of the observatory, where groundbreaking work in astronomy, including SETI (the search for extraterrestrial intelligence) continues. ⊠ *Rte. 625,* ☎ *787/878–2612.* ⊡ *Free.* ☼ *Tues.–Fri. 2–3, Sun. 1–4:30.*

㊼ Boquerón. This tiny, funky, pastel village has sidewalk oyster vendors, bars, restaurants serving fresh seafood, and several of the standard T-shirt shops. There are also diving and snorkeling tours at the Boquerón Dive Shop on Main Street. Boquerón's balneario is one of the best beaches on the island. Parking is $1 per car, and two-room rustic cabins are for rent (☎ 787/724–2500, ext. 130 or 131). ⊠ *Rte. 101.*

㊺ Cabo Rojo. Once a pirates' hangout, this town is now a favorite resort area of Puerto Ricans. The area has long stretches of white-sand beaches on the clear, calm Caribbean Sea, as well as many seafood restaurants, bars, and hotels. There are also several paradores in the region. ⊠ *Rte. 102.*

㊳ Caguana Indian Ceremonial Park. This area was used 800 years ago by the Taíno tribes for recreation and worship. Mountains surround a 13-acre site planted with royal palms and guava. According to Spanish historians, the Taínos played a game similar to soccer, and in this park there are 10 courts bordered by cobbled walkways. There are also stone monoliths, some with colorful petroglyphs; a small museum; and a souvenir shop. ⊠ *Rte. 111, Km 12.3,* ☎ *787/894–7325.* ⊡ *Free.* ☼ *Daily 9–4:30.*

44   **Mayagüez.** Puerto Rico's third-largest city has a population approaching 100,000. Although bypassed by the mania for restoration that saw Ponce and Old San Juan spruced up for the Columbus quincentennial, Mayagüez is graced by some lovely turn-of-the-century architecture, such as the landmark Art Deco Teatro Yagüez and the Plaza de Colón.

☙   North of town visit the **Mayagüez Zoo,** a 45-acre tropical compound that's home to about 500 animals. In addition to Bengal tigers, reptiles, and birds, there's a lake and a children's playground. ✉ *Rte. 108 at Barrio Miradero,* ☎ *787/834–8110.* ☜ *$1; parking $1.* ⊙ *Wed.–Sun. 9–4.*

43   **Mona Island.** Fifty miles west of Mayagüez in the turbulent shark-infested Mona Passage, Mona Island is nicknamed the Galápagos of the Caribbean, thanks to the plethora of endangered and unique indigenous species that call it home. The variety of marine and bird life is especially breathtaking. The coastline is rimmed with imposing limestone cliffs up to 200 feet high pocked with caves that are said to contain buried treasure; the many perfectly preserved Taíno hieroglyphs and rock paintings there are of great archaeological value.

Access to the island is only via private plane or boat. Very limited camping facilities are available on the pristine beaches. Call the Department of Natural Resources for information and camping reservations (☎ 787/723–1616 or 787/721–5495).

48   **Phosphorescent Bay.** The fishing village of **La Parguera,** an area of simple seafood restaurants, mangrove cays, and small islands, lies south of San Germán at the end of Route 304. This is an excellent scuba-diving area, but the main attraction is Phosphorescent Bay. Boats tour the bay, where microscopic dinoflagellates (marine plankton) light up like Christmas trees when disturbed by any kind of movement. The phenomenon can be seen only on moonless nights. Boats leave for the hour-long trip nightly between 7:30 and 12:30, depending on demand, and the trip costs $8 per person. You can also rent or charter a small boat to explore the numerous cays.

49 **Ponce.** From San Germán (☞ *below*), Route 2 traverses splendid peaks and valleys; pastel houses cling to the sides of steep green hills. The Cordillera Central mountains run parallel to Route 2 here and provide a stunning backdrop to the drive. East of Yauco, the road dips and sweeps right along the Caribbean and into Ponce.

Puerto Rico's second-largest city (population 300,000) underwent a massive restoration in preparation for its 300th anniversary, celebrated in 1996, of the city's first settlement.

The town's 19th-century style has been recaptured with pink marble-bordered sidewalks, gas lamps, painted trolleys, and horse-drawn carriages. You have not seen a firehouse until you've seen the red-and-black-striped **Parque de Bombas,** a structure built in 1882 for an exposition and converted to a firehouse the following year. The city hired architect Pablo Ojeda O'Neill to restore it, and it is now a museum of Ponce's history, which, not surprisingly, has a display of Fire Brigade memorabilia. ⊠ *Plaza Las Delicias,* ☎ *787/284–4141, ext. 342.* ⊑ *Free.* ☉ *Wed.–Mon. 9:30–6.*

Ponce's charm stems from a combination of neoclassical, Ponce Creole, and art-deco styles. The tiny streets lined with wrought-iron balconies are reminiscent of New Orleans's French Quarter. Stop in and pick up information about this seaside city at the columned **Casa Armstrong-Poventud,** the home of the Institute of Puerto Rican Culture and a Tourism Information Office, open weekdays 8–noon and 1–4:30 (use the side entrance). Stroll around the **Plaza Las Delicias,** with its perfectly pruned India-laurel fig trees, graceful fountains, gardens, and park benches. View **Our Lady of Guadelupe Cathedral** (masses are held daily), and walk down Calles Isabel and Christina to see turn-of-the-century wooden houses with wrought-iron balconies.

Two superlative examples of early-20th-century architecture house the **Ponce History Museum** (Museo de la Historia de Ponce), where 10 rooms of exhibits vividly re-create Ponce's golden years, providing especially fascinating glimpses into the worlds of culture, high finance, and journalism during the 19th century. ⊠ *53 Calle Isabel,* ☎ *787/844–7071.* ⊑ *$3.* ☉ *Mon. and Wed.–Fri. 10–5, weekends 10–6.*

Continue as far as Calles Mayor and Christina to the white stucco **La Perla Theater,** with its Corinthian columns. Be sure to allow time to visit the **Ponce Museum of Art** (Museo de Arte de Ponce). The architecture alone is worth seeing: The modern, two-story building designed by Edward Durell Stone (who designed New York's Museum of Modern Art) has seven interconnected hexagons, glass cupolas, and a pair of curved staircases. The collection includes late Renaissance and Baroque works from Italy, France, and Spain, as well as contemporary art by Puerto Ricans. ⊠ *Av. Las Américas,* ☎ *787/848–0505.* ▧ *$3.* ☉ *Daily 10–5.*

Another fine museum is **Castillo Serrallés,** a splendid Spanish Revival mansion perched on El Vigía Hill, with smashing views of Ponce and the Caribbean. This former residence of the Serrallés family, owners of the Don Q rum distillery, has been restored with a mix of original furnishings and antiques that recall the era of the sugar barons, including a baronial dining room with heavy carved mahogany and wrought-iron doors. A short film details the history of the sugar and rum industries. The unusual, rather ugly 100-foot-tall cross (La Cruceta del Vigía) looming behind the museum is being restored; when finished (a completion date had not been set at press time), visitors will be able to climb to its observation tower. ⊠ *El Vigía Hill,* ☎ *787/259–1774.* ▧ *$3.* ☉ *Tues.–Sun. 10–5.*

There are two intriguing historical sights just outside the city. **Hacienda Buena Vista** is a 19th-century coffee plantation, restored by the Conservation Trust of Puerto Rico, with much of the authentic machinery and furnishings intact. Reservations are required for the 90-minute tours; tours in English are given on request (in advance) once a day. ⊠ *Rte. 10, Km 16.8, north of Ponce,* ☎ *787/722–5882 weekdays, 787/848–7020 weekends.* ▧ *$5.* ☉ *Wed.–Fri. open to tour groups; Fri.–Sun. open to public.*

The **Tibes Indian Ceremonial Center** is the oldest cemetery in the Caribbean. It is a treasure trove of pre-Taíno ruins and burials, dating from AD 300 to AD 700. Some archaeologists, noting the symmetrical arrangement of stone pillars, surmise the cemetery may have been of great religious significance. The complex includes a detailed re-creation

of a Taíno village and a museum. ⊠ *Rte. 503, Km 2.7,* ☏
787/840–2255. ⊡ *$2.* ☉ *Wed.–Sun. 9–4.*

42 **Rincón.** Located along Route 115, one of the island's most
scenic areas of rolling hills dotted with pastel-colored
houses, Rincón is perched on a hill and overlooks its beach,
which was the site of the World Surfing Championship in
1968. Skilled surfers flock to Rincón during the winter, when
the water is rough and challenging. The town is also increasingly popular with divers. Locals boast that the best
diving and snorkeling in Puerto Rico (and some even say
the Caribbean) is off the Rincón coast, particularly around
the offshore island of Desecheo, a federal wildlife preserve.
Whale-watching is another draw for this town; humpback
whales winter off the coast from December through February. ⊠ *Rte. 115.*

39 **Río Camuy Cave Park.** This 268-acre reserve contains one
of the world's largest cave networks. Guided tours take you
on a tram down through dense tropical vegetation to the
entrance of the cave, where you continue on foot over underground trails, ramps, and bridges. The caves, sinkholes,
and subterranean streams are all spectacular (the world's
second-largest underground river runs through here), but
this trip is not for the claustrophobic. Be sure to call ahead;
the tours allow only a limited number of people. ⊠ *Rte.
129, Km 18.9,* ☏ *787/898–3100 or 787/756–5555.* ⊡ *$10;
parking $1.* ☉ *Tues.–Sun. 8–4. Last tour starts at 3:50.*

46 **San Germán.** This quiet and colorful Old World town is
home to the oldest intact church under the U.S. flag. Built
in 1606, **Porta Coeli** (Gates of Heaven) overlooks one of
the town's two plazas (where the townspeople continue the
Spanish tradition of promenading at night). The church is
now a museum of religious art, housing 18th- and 19th-
century paintings and wooden statues. ⊠ *Rte. 102,* ☏
787/892–5845. ⊡ *Free.* ☉ *Tues.–Sun. 9–noon and 1–4.*

3 Dining

HE QUALITY OF RESTAURANTS on Puerto Rico is among the best in the Caribbean. In San Juan you'll find everything from Italian to Thai, as well as superb local eateries serving *comidas criollas* (traditional Caribbean-Creole meals). Many of San Juan's best restaurants, such as Pikayo, Chayote, and Augusto's, are in small, lesser-known hotels. If you're staying in the capital, by all means venture out and sample the wealth of options available. Wherever you go, it is *always* a good idea to make reservations in the busy season, from mid-November through April.

Puerto Rican cooking emphasizes local vegetables: Plantains are cooked a hundred different ways—*tostones* (fried green), *amarillos* (baked ripe), and chips. Rice and beans with tostones or amarillos are basic accompaniments to every dish. Locals cook white rice with *habichuelas* (red beans), *achiote* (annatto seeds), or saffron; brown rice with *gandules* (pigeon peas); and *morro* (black rice) with *frijoles negros* (black beans). Garbanzos and white beans are served in many daily specials. A wide assortment of yams is served baked, fried, stuffed, boiled, mashed, and whole. *Sofrito*—a garlic, onion, sweet pepper, coriander, oregano, and tomato puree—is used as a base for practically everything.

Beef, chicken, pork, and seafood are all rubbed with *adobo,* a garlic-oregano marinade, before cooking. *Arroz con pollo* (chicken with rice), *sancocho* (beef and tuber soup), *asopao* (a soupy rice with chicken or seafood), and *encebollado* (steak smothered in onions) are all typical plates.

Fritters, also popular, are served in snack places along the highways as well as at cocktail parties. You may find *empanadillas* (stuffed fried turnovers), *surrullitos* (cheese-stuffed corn sticks), *alcapurias* (stuffed green banana croquettes), and *bacalaitos* (codfish fritters).

Local *pan de agua* is an excellent French loaf bread, best hot out of the oven. It is also good toasted and should be tried in the *Cubano* sandwich (roast pork, ham, Swiss cheese, pickles, and mustard).

Local desserts include flans, puddings, and fruit pastes served with native white cheese. Homegrown mangoes and papayas are sweet, and *pan de azucar* (sugar bread) pineapples make the best juice on the market. Fresh *parcha* (passion fruit), *guarapo* (sugarcane), and *guanabana* (a fruit similar to papaya) juice are also sold cold from trucks along the highway. Puerto Rican coffee is excellent served espresso-black or generously cut *con leche* (with hot milk).

To sample local cuisine, consult the listing of *mesones gastrónomicos* in the *¿Qué Pasa?* guide. These are restaurants cited by the government for preserving island culinary traditions and maintaining high standards.

The best frozen piña coladas are served at the Caribe Hilton and the Hyatt Dorado Beach, although local legend has it that the birthplace of the piña colada is the Gran Hotel El Convento. Rum can be mixed with cola (known as a *cuba libre*), soda, tonic, juices, water, served on the rocks, or even straight up. Puerto Rican rums range from light white mixers to dark, aged sipping liqueurs. Look for Bacardi, Don Q, Ron Rico, Palo Viejo, and Barrilito.

What to Wear

The dress code for restaurants in Puerto Rico varies greatly. The price category of a restaurant is usually a good indicator of its formality. For less expensive places, anything but beachwear is generally fine. Ritzier hotel dining rooms and expensive eateries will expect collared shirts for men and chic attire for women, although jacket and tie requirements are rare. However, Puerto Ricans enjoy dressing up for dinner, so chances are you'll never feel overdressed.

CATEGORY	COST*
$$$$	over $45
$$$	$30–$45
$$	$15–$30
$	under $15

per person, excluding drinks and service

Old San Juan

$$$$ ✕ **Chef Marisoll.** Set off a Venetianesque courtyard surrounded by ornate balconies (you can dine inside or out), this dark-wooded, high-ceilinged restaurant serves gourmet international cuisine. Start with a small duck caesar salad or a cream of exotic wild mushroom soup. Then feast on a beef tenderloin or a fillet of salmon. For dessert, try Chef Marisoll's specialty, a crème caramel. ⊠ *202 Calle Cristo,* ☎ *787/725–7454. AE, D, MC, V. Closed Mon. No lunch Sun.*

$$$$ ✕ **Il Perugino.** The best Italian restaurant in Old San Juan,
★ this small and intimate eatery set in a 200-year-old building stresses attentive service and delicious Italian cuisine. Classic carpaccios, scallops with porcini mushrooms and other exotic salads, homemade pastas like black fettuccine with crayfish and baby eels, hearty main courses such as rack of lamb with red wine sauce and aromatic herbs, and desserts like a killer *tiramisù* make this a must for serious gourmets. An excellent wine cellar, housed in the former cistern, completes the experience. ⊠ *105 Calle Cristo,* ☎ *787/722–5481. AE, MC, V.*

$$$–$$$$ ✕ **La Chaumière.** Reminiscent of an inn in the French provinces, this intimate restaurant with black-and-white floors, heavy wood beams, and floral curtains serves onion soup, oysters Rockefeller, rack of lamb, scallops Provençale, and veal Oscar (layered with lobster and asparagus in béarnaise sauce) in addition to daily specials. ⊠ *367 Calle Tetuan,* ☎ *787/722–3330. AE, DC, MC, V. Closed Sun. No lunch.*

$$–$$$ ✕ **Amadeus.** In an atmosphere of gentrified Old San Juan,
★ this charming restaurant offers a nouvelle Caribbean menu. The front dining room is attractive—whitewashed walls, dark wood, white napery, ceiling fans, and a trendy, pretty crowd to match—but go through the outside passage to the back dining room where printed cloths, candles, and exposed brick make for even more romantic dining. The roster of appetizers includes buffalo wings and plantain mousse with shrimp. Chicken breast stuffed with sun-dried tomatoes, cheese ravioli with a goat-cheese-and-walnut sauce, and Cajun-grilled mahimahi are a few of the delectable entrées. ⊠ *106 Calle San Sebastián,* ☎ *787/722–8635. AE, MC, V. Closed Mon.*

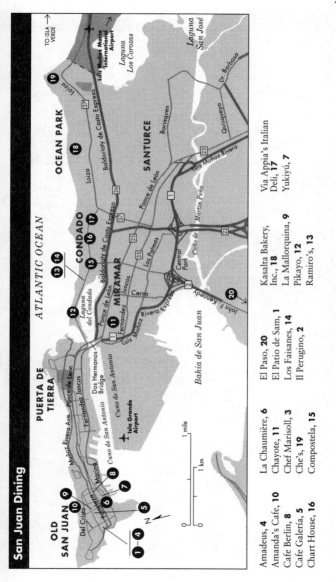

San Juan Dining

TO ISLA VERDE →

Luis Muñoz Marín International Airport →

Laguna Los Corozas

Laguna San José

ATLANTIC OCEAN

OCEAN PARK

SANTURCE

CONDADO

MIRAMAR

PUERTA DE TIERRA

OLD SAN JUAN

Laguna del Condado

Bahía de San Juan

Dos Hermanos Bridge

Isla Grande Airport

JOHN F. KENNEDY →

N

1 mile

1 km

Amadeus, **4**
Amanda's Cafe, **10**
Cafe Berlin, **8**
Cafe Galería, **5**
Chart House, **16**

La Chaumière, **6**
Chayote, **11**
Chef Marisoll, **3**
Che's, **19**
Compostela, **15**

El Paso, **20**
El Patio de Sam, **1**
Los Faisanes, **14**
Il Perugino, **2**

Kasalta Bakery,
Inc., **18**
La Mallorquina, **9**
Pikayo, **12**
Ramiro's, **13**

Via Appia's Italian
Deli, **17**
Yukiyú, **7**

Puerto Rico Dining

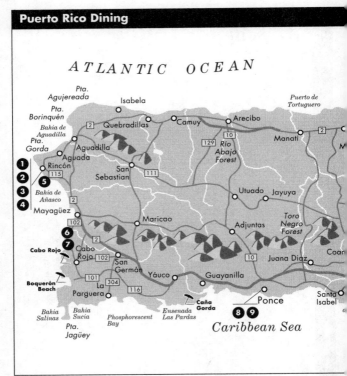

Anchor's Inn, **10**

Black Eagle, **4**

El Bohio, **7**

La Casona de
Serafin, **6**

Horned Dorset
Primavera, **5**

Lazy Parrot, **3**

Lupita's, **8**

El Molina del
Quijote
Restaurante, **1**

Pastrami
Palace, **2**

Restaurant El
Ancla, **9**

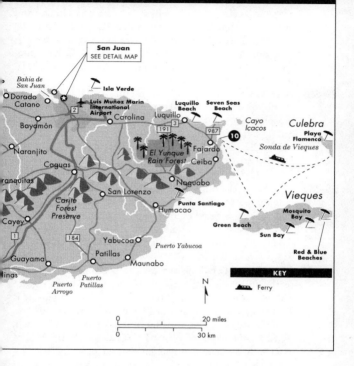

San Juan
SEE DETAIL MAP

Bahia de
San Juan

Isla Verde

Dorado
Catano

Luis Muñoz Marin
International
Airport

Carolina

Luquillo

Luquillo
Beach

Seven Seas
Beach

Cayo
Icacos

Culebra

Playa
Flamenco

Bayamón

Naranjito

Sonda de Vieques

Caguas

El Yunque
Rain Forest

Fajardo

Ceiba

Naguabo

Vieques

ranquitas

San Lorenzo

Carite
Forest
Preserve

Humacao

Punta Santiago

Mosquito
Bay

Cayey

Green Beach

Sun Bay

Yabucoa

Red & Blue
Beaches

Guayama

Patillas

Puerto Yabucoa

Maunabo

linas

Puerto
Arroyo

Puerto
Patillas

N

KEY

Ferry

0   20 miles

0   30 km

$$–$$$ ✕ **Cafe Galería.** This stylish, airy restaurant, with marble floors, white walls, and dark wood accents, is centered around a skylit atrium. Chef Figueroa prepares Italian and international cuisine featuring fresh pastas and sauces (you mix and match), risottos, and seafood dishes as well as delicious local desserts like flan, *arroz con dulce* (rice pudding), and kiwi tart. ⊠ 205 *Calle San Justo*, ☎ 787/725–0478. *AE, MC, V. Closed Sun.*

$$–$$$ ✕ **La Mallorquina.** The oldest restaurant in Puerto Rico (it is said to date from 1848) is recommended more for its atmosphere than for its food. Pale pink walls and whirring ceiling fans are pleasant, and the nattily attired wait staff is friendly. The food is good but basic Puerto Rican and Spanish fare, such as asopao and paella. ⊠ 207 *Calle San Justo*, ☎ 787/722–3261. *AE, MC, V.*

$$–$$$ ✕ **Yukiyú.** The only Japanese restaurant in Old San Juan,
★ it manages to serve some of the best Japanese food in Puerto Rico under the supervision of Chef Igarashi. Those craving a sushi bar should make a beeline for this establishment, as sushi is a specialty, along with teppan yaki. ⊠ 311 *Recinto Sur*, ☎ 787/721–0653. *AE, MC, V.*

$$ ✕ **Amanda's Cafe.** This airy café, across from San Cristóbal on the north side of the city, offers seating inside or out with a view of the Atlantic and the old city wall. The cuisine is Mexican, French, and Caribbean, and the nachos, refreshing fruit frappés, and margaritas are the best in town. ⊠ 424 *Calle Norzagaray*, ☎ 787/722–0187. *AE, MC, V.*

$–$$ ✕ **El Patio de Sam.** A warm dark-wood and faux-brick interior and a wide selection of beers make Sam's a popular late-night gathering place. The menu is mostly steaks and seafood, with a few native dishes like asopao mixed in. Try the Samueles Special pizza—mozzarella, tomato sauce, beef, pepperoni, and black olives: It feeds two or three adults. The dessert flans melt in your mouth. ⊠ 102 *Calle San Sebastián*, ☎ 787/723–1149. *AE, D, DC, MC, V.*

$ ✕ **Cafe Berlin.** This casual café, bakery, and delicatessen has
★ outdoor seating overlooking the Plaza Colón. Tasty vegetarian fare prevails—try one of the creative salads. Nonvegetarian dishes are also available. The Cafe's pastries, desserts, fresh juices, and organic coffee are the perfect elixir to a day of touring Old San Juan. ⊠ 407 *Calle San Francisco*, ☎ 787/722–5205. *MC, V.*

San Juan

$$$$ ✕ **Compostela.** Contemporary Spanish food and a serious
★ 9,000-bottle wine cellar are the draws to Compostela, a
restaurant with a dark-wood interior and many plants.
Specialties include mushroom pâté and Port *pastelillo* (meat-
filled pastries), grouper fillet with scallops in salsa verde,
rack of lamb, duck with kiwi sauce, and paella. This is a
favorite restaurant with the local dining elite, and it is hon-
ored yearly in local competitions. ⊠ *106 Av. Condado, San-*
turce, ☎ *787/724–6088. AE, DC, MC, V. Closed Sun.*

$$$$ ✕ **Pikayo.** Chef Wilo Benet is one of the darlings in the
★ foodie firmament, thanks to his artful fusion of classic
French, Caribbean Creole, and California nouvelle cuisine
with definite Puerto Rican flair. The beautifully presented
dishes, which change regularly, are a feast for the eye as
well as the palate. Your meal might consist of tostones stuffed
with oven-dried tomatoes, followed by *monfongo* (spiced,
mashed green plantains topped with saffron shrimp) or a
hearty land-crab stew. More traditional and equally delicious dishes are also available. The decor is smartly contemporary, with lots of black-and-white accents and
comfortable banquettes, and the service is very attentive.
⊠ *Tanama Princess Hotel, 1 Calle Joffre, Condado,* ☎ *787/*
721–6194. AE, MC, V. Closed Sun. and Mon. No lunch
Sat.

$$$$ ✕ **Ramiro's.** Step into a soft sea green dining room for some
★ imaginative Castilian cuisine. Chef-owner Jesus Ramiro is
known for his artistic presentation: flower-shape peppers
filled with fish mousse, a mix of seafood caught under a
vegetable net, roast duckling with sugarcane honey, and,
if you can stand more, a kiwi dessert sculpted to resemble
twin palms. ⊠ *1106 Av. Magdalena, Condado,* ☎ *787/721–*
9049. AE, DC, MC, V. No lunch Sat.

$$$–$$$$ ✕ **Chayote.** Chef Alfredo Ayala, a champion of the latest
★ trends in Puerto Rican and Caribbean cuisine, has created
a sensation with this restaurant. Slightly off the beaten
path in Miramar, this elegant and chic eatery of earthen tones
and contemporary Puerto Rican art is an "in" spot to eat
among the San Juan cognoscenti. The chef fuses haute in-
ternational cuisine with tropical panache. Appetizers include
sopas del dias (soups of the day) made with local produce

like yuca and yams, chayote stuffed with prosciutto, cheese and tomatoes in a tempura batter, and corn tamales with shrimp in coconut sauce. Half of the entrées on the menu are seafood dishes, including pan-seared tuna with Asian ginger sauce and black grouper fillet in a vegetable fricassee sauce with Gouda cheese fritters. Classic meat dishes like fillet of beef and rack of lamb are also available. The ginger flan and the almond floating island in rum custard sauce are musts for dessert. ⊠ *Hotel Olimpo Court, 603 Av. Miramar, Miramar,* ☎ *787/722–9385. AE, MC, V. Closed Sun.*

$$$–$$$$ ✕ **Los Faisanes.** This Continental stunner is one of San Juan's most distinguished eateries. Mahogany doorways, faux-Tiffany lamps, crisp white and ecru napery, and Bernadaud china set a refined tone, carried through by the equally elegant cuisine. Feast on roast duck with guava and cinnamon, veal chops with scallion and mushroom sauce, and wonderfully light soufflés. ⊠ *1108 Av. Magdalena, Condado,* ☎ *787/725–2801. AE, MC, V.*

$$$ ✕ **Chart House.** It's no secret that the graceful veranda of this restored Ashford mansion across from the Marriott is a perfect spot for cocktails, and a lively crowd gathers here in the evening. The upstairs open-air dining rooms are splashed with bright marine-themed artwork. The menu includes prime rib, steak, shrimp teriyaki, Hawaiian chicken, and the signature dessert: mud pie. ⊠ *1214 Av. Ashford, Condado,* ☎ *787/728–0110. AE, D, DC, MC, V. No lunch.*

$$ ✕ **Che's.** Juicy *churrasco* (barbecued steaks), lemon chicken, and grilled sweetbreads are specialties at this casual Argentinean restaurant. The hamburgers are huge, and the french fries are fresh. The Chilean and Argentinean wine list is also decent. ⊠ *35 Calle Caoba, Punta Las Marias,* ☎ *787/726–7202. AE, D, DC, MC, V.*

$ ✕ **El Paso.** This family-run restaurant serves genuine Creole food seasoned for a local following. Specialties include asopao, pork chops, and breaded *empanadas* (meat pastries). There's always tripe on Saturday and arroz con pollo on Sunday. ⊠ *405 Av. De Diego, Puerto Nuevo,* ☎ *787/ 781–3399. AE, DC, MC, V.*

$ ✕ **Kasalta Bakery, Inc.** Make your selection from rows of
★   display cases offering a seemingly endless array of tempt-

ing treats. Walk up to the counter and order from an assortment of sandwiches (try the Cubano), meltingly tender octopus salad, savory *caldo gallego* (a soup jammed with fresh vegetables, sausage, and potatoes), cold drinks, strong café con leche, and luscious pastries. ⊠ *1966 Calle McLeary, Ocean Park,* ☎ *787/727–7340. AE, MC, V.*

$ ✕ **Via Appia's Italian Deli.** The only true sidewalk café in the Condado, this eatery serves pizzas, sandwiches, cold beer, and pitchers of sangria. It is a good place to people-watch. The staff is somewhat grumpy, however. ⊠ *1350 Av. Ashford, Condado,* ☎ *787/725–8711. AE, MC, V.*

Out on the Island

Cabo Rojo

$$ ✕ **La Casona de Serafin.** This informal, ocean-side bistro is a *mesón gastronómique* and specializes in steaks, seafood, and Puerto Rican *criolla* (Creole) dishes. The indoor dining room has bleached walls, mahogany furniture, and subdued red napery. Try the tostones, asopao, and surrullitos, and follow up with the pumpkin-custard dessert. The somewhat dilapidated palm-fringed patio sits right on the beach, so you can listen to the waves lap the shore. ⊠ *Hwy. 102, Km 9,* ☎ *787/851–0066. AE, MC, V.*

$–$$ ✕ **El Bohío.** A local favorite, this informal restaurant 15 minutes south of Mayagüez serves steak and a variety of seafood—all cooked just about any way you want it. You can dine on the large, enclosed wooden deck that juts out over the sea or in the dining room inside. ⊠ *Hwy. 102, Playa Joyuda,* ☎ *787/851–2755. AE, DC, MC, V.*

Fajardo

$–$$ ✕ **Anchor's Inn.** From the windows of this unadorned seaside eatery, you can watch the flotillas of brightly colored yachts and fishing boats in Fajardo harbor. The latter must head straight for the restaurant with their catch, for the seafood is as fresh and succulent as it gets. A *mesón gastronómico,* Anchor's Inn specializes in such Puerto Rican dishes as surrullitos, asopao, and lobster *mofongo* (green plantains stuffed with lobster). There are seven guest rooms upstairs. ⊠ *Rte. 987, Km 2.4,* ☎ *787/863–7200. AE, MC, V. Closed Tues.*

Ponce

$$ ✕ **Restaurant El Ancla.** The seafood and Puerto Rican spe-
cialties here are served with tostones, *papas fritas* (french
fries), and garlic bread. The menu ranges from lobster and
shrimp to chicken, beef, and asopao. The piña coladas, with
or without rum, and the flan are especially good. ⊠ *Av.
Hostos Final 9, Playa-Ponce,* ☎ *787/840–2450. AE, DC,
MC, V.*

$ ✕ **Lupita's.** A fine mariachi band patrols the mezzanine and
courtyard of this festive Mexican restaurant Thursday
through Sunday nights. The handsome arched dining room
has an Aztec decor, with ponchos and serapes hung on the
walls for added color. The food—Mexican-American stan-
dards like nachos, tacos, and chicken mole—is quite good,
the margaritas and shooters even better, and the ambience
festive. ⊠ *Calle Isabel 60,* ☎ *787/848–8808. AE, MC, V.*

Rincón

$$$–$$$$ ✕ **Horned Dorset Primavera.** Tucked away on the west
★ coast of the island in a posh hotel of the same name, this
is the finest food you'll encounter outside of San Juan.
Owners Harold Davies and Kingsley Wratten take their din-
ing room very seriously. The menu is printed in two lan-
guages, French and Spanish, even though most of the
clientele is American (the waiters save the day). Although
tropical accents appear here and there, the cuisine is heav-
ily Cordon Bleu–influenced: Filet mignon in a mushroom
sauce, braised lamb in red wine, and grilled fish du jour are
de rigueur here. A five-course, prix-fixe menu is available
for $48 per person. ⊠ *Rte. 429, Km 3, Box 1132,* ☎
787/823–4030 or 787/823–4050. AE, MC, V.

$$ ✕ **Black Eagle.** The inconsistent quality of the food here
hasn't dimmed its status as a Rincón dining landmark. It's
on the water's edge, and you dine on the veranda, listen-
ing to the lapping waves. The steak-and-seafood menu lists
breaded conch fritters, a fresh fish of the day, lobster, and
imported prime meats. ⊠ *Hwy. 413, Km 1,* ☎ *787/823–
3510. AE, DC, MC, V.*

$$ ✕ **El Molino del Quijote Restaurante.** Amid beautifully
landscaped gardens just off the beach, this festive, color-
ful restaurant with tile-topped tables and local artwork serves
Spanish and Puerto Rican cuisine. Try the *bolas de pescado*

(fish balls) appetizer and one of the paellas as an entrée, or combine several appetizers for a meal. The sangria is highly recommended. Two one-bedroom cabanas are available to rent. ⊠ *Rte. 429, Km 3.3,* ☎ *787/823–4010. AE, MC, V. Closed Mon.–Thurs.*

$–$$ ✕ **Lazy Parrot.** Highly regarded by locals in Rincón for its fresh mahimahi, filet mignon, and homemade desserts, this little restaurant is also an art gallery and guest house. Perched in the hills, with mountain and ocean views, this is great place to kick back and listen to the ever-present sound of the coquis. It's only open on weekends in the summer. ⊠ *Rte. 413, Km 4.1, Barrio Puntas,* ☎ *787/823–5654. AE, MC, V. Closed Mon. in winter.*

$ ✕ **Pastrami Palace.** A favorite ex-pat hangout, this friendly, small restaurant and lunch counter in downtown Rincón serves up American basics from omelets, pancakes, and sandwiches to homemade pies, ice cream, and excellent coffee. The colorful decor includes local artwork, and there's a small library for lunchtime reading. An outdoor café is called (groan) the Garden of Eatin. ⊠ *Calle Parque,* ☎ *787/823–0102. No credit cards. No dinner.*

4 Lodging

In case you want to be welcomed there.

We're here to see that you're always welcomed at establishments everywhere. That's why millions of people carry the American Express® Card — for peace of mind, confidence, and security, around the world or just around the corner.

do more ®

AMERICAN
EXPRESS

Cards

In case you're running low.

We're here to help with more than 118,000 Express Cash locations around the world. In order to enroll, just call American Express before you start your vacation.

do more

AMERICAN EXPRESS

Express Cash

And just in case.

We're here with American Express® Travelers Cheques and Cheques *for Two*® They're the safest way to carry money on your vacation and the surest way to get a refund, practically anywhere, anytime. Another way we help you...

do more®

AMERICAN EXPRESS

Travelers Cheques

CCOMMODATIONS ON PUERTO RICO
come in all shapes and sizes. Self-
contained luxury resorts cover hun-
dreds of acres. San Juan's high-rise beachfront hotels
likewise cater to the cruise-ship and casino crowd; several
target the business traveler. Out on the island, the govern-
ment-sponsored paradores are lodgings modeled after
Spain's successful parador system. Some are rural inns,
some offer motel-style (no-frill) apartments, and some are
large hotels. They are required to meet certain standards,
such as proximity to a sightseeing attraction or beach and
a kitchen serving native cuisine. Parador prices range from
$50 to $125 for a double room. Reservations for all
paradores can be made by calling 800/443–0266 in the
United States, 787/721–2884 in San Juan, or 800/981–7575
elsewhere in Puerto Rico. They are a phenomenal bargain
but tend to get noisy and raucous on weekends, when families descend from the cities for a minivacation.

Most hotels in Puerto Rico operate on the European Plan
(EP). In some larger hotels, however, packages are available that include several or all meals, while others offer all-
inclusive deals. Also, beware when booking hotels outside
of San Juan that rates most often do not include airport transfers. Be sure to ask if the hotel offers transportation, the
cost, and if advance arrangements are necessary.

CATEGORY	COST*
$$$$	over $225
$$$	$150–$225
$$	$75–$150
$	under $75

*All prices are for a standard double room for two, exclud-
ing 7% tax (9% for hotels with casinos) and 10%–15% service charge.*

Old San Juan

$$–$$$ 🏨 **Gallery Inn.** Owners Jan D'Esopo and Manuco Gandia
★ restored this rambling, classically Spanish house, one of the
oldest private residences in the area, and turned it into an

inn. It's full of quirky architectural details—winding, uneven stairs; private balconies; a music room with a Steinway grand piano; lots of public rooms, areas, and decks to hide out with a book; and small interior gardens. The rooms are individually decorated and have telephones but no televisions; most are air-conditioned. Among the best rooms are Terrasina and Jonathan (all the rooms are named after Jan's children and grandchildren). Views from the rooftop patio are some of the best in the old city—a panorama of the El Morro and San Cristóbal forts and the Atlantic. Galería San Juan, a small gallery and working studio in the inn, features work in various medias by Jan D'Esopo, Bruno Lucchesi, and Teresa Spinner. Sculptures and silk-screen prints fill nearly every nook and cranny of the inn. There's even a package available that combines a five-night stay with the creation of your portrait bust. There is no restaurant, but meals can be cooked for groups upon request. ⊠ *204–206 Calle Norzagaray, 00901,* ☎ *787/722–1808,* FAX *787/724–7360. 16 rooms and suites. Self-service bar. AE, MC, V. CP.*

San Juan

$$$$ 🏨 **Caribe Hilton International.** Built in 1949, this property
  ★   occupies 17 acres on Puerta de Tierra. Rooms have been modernized and refurbished over the years and have a crisp, pastel decor and balconies with ocean or lagoon views; the higher the floor, the better the view. The Tower rooms, however, could use freshening up. Be sure to ask for a room in the main part of the hotel. Executive levels provide services such as private check-in and checkout, complimentary evening cocktails, and complimentary Continental breakfast for business travelers. The spacious atrium lobby—a hub of activity—is decorated with rose marble, waterfalls, and lavish tropical plants. Restaurants include Batey del Pescador for seafood and Peacock Paradise for Chinese cuisine. The hotel has San Juan's only private beach, complete with a boardwalk at its edge. ⊠ *Box 1872, San Juan 00902,* ☎ *787/721–0303 or 800/468–8585,* FAX *787/724–6992. 672 rooms and suites. 6 restaurants, air-conditioning, 2 pools, 6 tennis courts, exercise room, racquetball, squash, beach, casino, business services. AE, D, DC, MC, V. EP, MAP.*

$$$$ 🏨 **Condado Plaza Hotel and Casino.** The Atlantic and the Condado Lagoon border this property. Two wings, appropriately named Ocean and Lagoon, are connected by an enclosed, elevated walkway over Avenida Ashford. Standard rooms have walk-in closets and separate dressing areas. There are a variety of suites, including spa suites with oversize Jacuzzis, and a fully equipped business center. The Plaza Club floor has 24-hour concierge service and a private lounge, and guests there receive complimentary Continental breakfast, afternoon hors d'oeuvres, and evening coffee. The Ocean wing sits on a small strip of public beach, and there are two pools. This is the sister hotel of the El San Juan resort, and guests have access to all the facilities there via a complimentary shuttle bus (the bus will also drop passengers off in Old San Juan). Dining options include Tony Roma's (a branch of the American chain) and an informal restaurant poolside. ⊠ *999 Av. Ashford, Condado 00902,* ☎ *787/721–1000 or 800/468–8588,* FAX *787/722–7955. 589 rooms and suites. 7 restaurants, 3 bars, air-conditioning, 5 pools (1 saltwater), hot tub, 2 tennis courts, health club, water-sports center, casino, business services. AE, D, DC, MC, V. EP, MAP.*

$$$$ 🏨 **El San Juan Hotel and Casino.** An immense chandelier
★ illuminates the hand-carved mahogany paneling, rose marble, and French tapestries in the huge lobby of this 12-acre resort on the Isla Verde beach. The casino is right off the lobby. You'll be hard pressed to decide if you want a suite in the main tower, with whirlpool bath and wet bar; a garden lanai room, with private patio and whirlpool bath; or a casita, with a sunken Roman bath. (Some of the tower rooms have no balcony or ocean view; be sure to check.) All rooms have CD player, three phones, TV with VCR, minibar, and walk-in closets with an iron and board. Dark rattan furnishings are complemented by rich carpets and tropical-print spreads and drapes. This luxurious hotel attracts a moneyed mix of international business and leisure travelers. The posh Dar Tiffany restaurant, an oasis of potted palms, etched glass, and Tiffany lamps, serves impeccable Continental fare. The intimate, romantic La Piccola Fontana is one of San Juan's better Italian restaurants. Don't miss the informal rooftop bar; watching the sunset from here is a splendid end to a day of sightseeing. ⊠ *Av.*

40

Puerto Rico Lodging

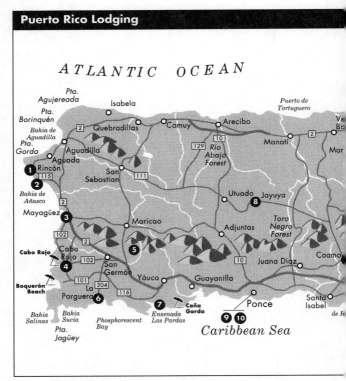

Casa del
Francés, **19**

El Conquistador
Resort and
Country
Club, **14**

Copamarina
Beach Resort, **7**

Crow's Nest, **16**

Hacienda
Tamarindo, **18**

Horned Dorset
Primavera, **1**

Hotel Melia, **10**

Hyatt Dorado
Beach, **13**

Hyatt Regency
Cerromar
Beach, **12**

Inn on the Blue
Horizon, **17**

Lemontree
Waterfront
Cottages, **2**

Mayagüez Hilton
and Casino, **3**

Palmas del
Mar, **15**

Parador Baños de
Coamo, **11**

Parador
Boquemar, **4**

Parador
Hacienda
Gripiñas, **8**

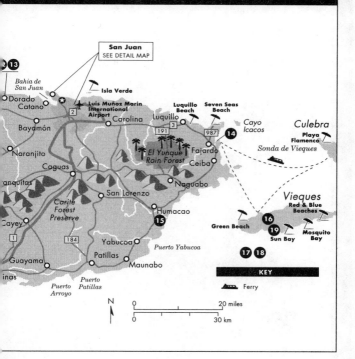

Parador Oasis, **5**
Parador Villa
Parguera, **6**
Ponce Hilton and
Casino, **9**

San Juan Lodging

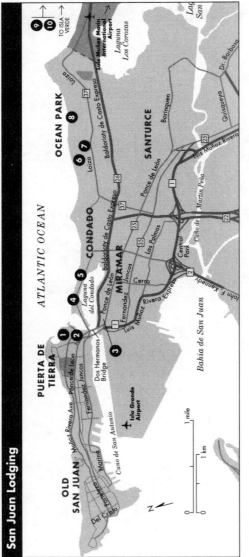

Caribe Hilton International, **1**
Condado Plaza Hotel and Casino, **4**
El San Juan Hotel and Casino, **9**

Excelsior, **3**
L'Habitation Beach Guest House, **7**
Hosteria del Mar, **8**
Numero Uno, **6**

Radisson Normandie, **2**
Sands Hotel and Casino, **10**
San Juan Marriott, **5**

Isla Verde, Box 2872, San Juan 00902, ☎ *787/791–1000 or 800/468–2818,* FAX *787/791–0390. 389 rooms. 5 restaurants, 8 bars, air-conditioning, minibars, accessible rooms for people with disabilities, no-smoking rooms, in-room VCRs, 2 pools (1 with swim-up bar), children's pool, 3 hot tubs, 3 tennis courts, health club, water-sports center, shops, casino, dance club, recreation room, concierge, business services, shuttle bus to Condado Plaza Hotel and Old San Juan. AE, DC, MC, V. EP, MAP.*

$$$$ **San Juan Marriott.** The red neon sign atop San Juan's
★ newest hotel is a beacon to its excellent Condado location.
The hotel opened in January 1995 and has been the keystone to the revival of tourism in the Condado. Rooms have soothing pastel carpeting, flowered spreads, attractive tropical artwork on the walls, and balconies overlooking the ocean, the pool, or both. The staff has been well trained and is both courteous and friendly. Restaurants include Tuscany, for northern Italian cuisine, and the more casual La Vista, popular for dining alfresco. On weekends, there's live entertainment in the enormous lobby, which, combined with the persistent ringing of slot machines from the adjoining casino, makes the area quite noisy (rooms are soundproofed). Gorgeous Condado beach is right outside, as is a large pool area. The hotel's spa/gym is the best of any resort in Puerto Rico. ⊠ *1309 Av. Ashford, San Juan 00907,* ☎ *787/722–7000 or 800/228–9290,* FAX *787/722–6800. 510 rooms, 15 suites. 3 restaurants, 2 lounges, air-conditioning, no-smoking rooms, pool, beauty salon, hot tub, sauna, 2 tennis courts, health club, casino, video games, children's programs, business services, meeting rooms. AE, D, DC, MC, V. EP, MAP, FAP.*

$$$$ **Sands Hotel and Casino.** One of Puerto Rico's largest
★ casinos glitters just off the lobby, stunning artwork from around the world grace the public rooms, and a huge free-form pool lies between the hotel and its beach. Rooms are air-conditioned and have tiny balconies (ask for one with an ocean view). The decor is basic tropical, with a green, peach, and white color scheme and white rattan furniture. The exclusive Plaza Club section is that rare executive level worth the added expense, offering garden suites, a masseuse, a small gym, and other enticements. ⊠ *187 Isla Verde Rd., Isla Verde 00979,* ☎ *787/791–6100 or 800/544–3008,* FAX

787/791–8525. 418 rooms. 4 restaurants, 2 lounges, air-conditioning, pool, water-sports center, casino, recreation room, concierge, business services. AE, D, DC, MC, V. EP.

$$$ 🏨 **Radisson Normandie.** This oceanfront, art-deco style hotel is a national landmark. It was built in 1939, in the shape of the fabled ocean liner of the same name. Rooms have minibars, cable TV, coffeemakers, and hair dryers; some have sunrooms. Additional frills and pampering can be found at the seventh-floor executive club, where you receive complimentary Continental breakfast and evening hors d'oeuvres. You can make reservations to use the tennis courts at the Hilton next door. ⊠ *Corner of Av. Muñoz Rivera and Av. Rosales, Puerta Tierra, Box 50059, San Juan 00902,* ☎ *787/729–2929 or 800/333–3333,* 🖷 *787/729–3083. 177 rooms. 2 restaurants, air-conditioning, lounge, pool, health club, jogging, scuba diving, snorkeling, boating, business services. AE, D, DC, MC, V. EP, MAP.*

$$ 🏨 **Excelsior.** Located across the Condado Lagoon in Miramar, the Excelsior is off the beaten path in a commercial area of the city and is popular with business travelers. Room decor here is standard hotel fare, but the rates are a good value. Each room has a phone, fridge, and a private bath with a hair dryer; some have kitchenettes. Fine carpets adorn the corridors, and sculptures decorate the lobby. Augusto's, one of the hotel's restaurants, is highly respected for its international cuisine. Complimentary coffee, newspaper, and shoe shine are offered each morning. ⊠ *801 Av. Ponce de León, Miramar 00907,* ☎ *787/721–7400 or 800/223–9815,* 🖷 *787/723–0068. 140 rooms. 2 restaurants, cocktail lounge, air-conditioning, refrigerators, pool, exercise room, beach shuttle, free parking. AE, DC, D, MC, V. EP.*

$$ 🏨 **Hosteria del Mar.** Right on the beach in Ocean Park, this ★ small, white inn/guest house is set in a residential neighborhood. It's a wonderful alternative to the hustle and bustle of the Condado or Old San Juan—you have to go down to the beach and look west to see the high-rises of the Condado looming in the distance. Rooms here are attractive and simple, with tropical prints and rattan furniture prevailing, and many have ocean views. Four apartments have kitchenettes. All accommodations are air-conditioned and come with cable TV and phones. The staff is courteous and helpful. A vegetarian-oriented restaurant is on the ground floor facing the trade winds and offers fabulous views of the wide beach in front. ✉ *1 Calle Tapia, Ocean Park 00911,* ☎ *787/727–3302,* ℻ *787/268–0772. 8 rooms, 4 apartments, 1 minisuite. Restaurant, air-conditioning. AE, DC, MC, V. EP.*

$$ 🏨 **Numero Uno.** Several years ago, former New Yorkers
★   Ester and Chris Laube bought this three-story, red-roofed guest house on the beach, spruced it up, and turned it into a very pleasant and comfortable accommodation. It's set in a quiet residential neighborhood, right in the middle of the nicest beach on San Juan. The simple but clean rooms offer double, queen-, or king-size beds and most are air-conditioned or have ceiling fans. A walled-in patio provides privacy for sunning or hanging out by the small pool. On the other side of the wall, a wide, sandy beach beckons. Beach chairs and towels are provided to guests. A bar and small restaurant borders the pool. ✉ *1 Calle Santa Ana, Ocean Park 00911,* ☎ *787/727–9687,* ℻ *787/726–5010. 12 rooms. Restaurant, bar, pool. AE, MC, V. CP.*

$–$$ 🏨 **L'Habitation Beach Guest House.** On the beach in Ocean
★   Park is this gay-oriented guest house with a definite French air. Owner Alain Tasca is from Paris by way of Guadeloupe and Key West. He has established a very relaxed ambience in this casual, eight-room accommodation. Rooms are well-sized, simple, and comfortable and all have air-conditioning and cable TV. Chambermaid Natasha sees to it that everything is kept clean and in its place and will chase after offenders who don't wash sand off their feet before entering the house. A bar and snack bar sit in a corner of a palm-shaded, sandy patio between the guest house and the beach. Beach chairs and towels are provided. Alain's margaritas will knock your sandals off. ✉ *1957 Calle Italia, Ocean Park 00911,* ☎ *787/727–2499,* ℻ *787/727–2599. 8 rooms. Bar, snack bar, air-conditioning, private beach. AE, MC, V. CP.*

Out on the Island

Cabo Rojo

$–$$ 🏨 **Parador Boquemar.** You can walk to the Boquerón public beach (one of the island's best) from this small parador at the end of Route 101. Rooms are comfortable. Each has air-conditioning, TV, minifridge, phone, and private bath and is decorated in the island uniform of tropical prints and rattan. Ask for a third-floor room with a balcony overlooking the water. La Cascada, a *mesón gastronomique,* is well known for its superior, traditional native cuisine. On weekends, the lounge is filled with live music. At press time, the parador was adding 20 new rooms. ⊠ *Box 133, Boquerón 00622,* ☎ *787/851–2158 or 800/443–0266,* 𝐅𝐀𝐗 *787/851– 7600. 64 rooms. Restaurant, lounge, air-conditioning, refrigerators, pool, coin laundry across street. AE, D, DC, MC, V. EP.*

Coamo

$ ⊞ **Parador Baños de Coamo.** On Route 546, Km 1, northeast of Ponce, this mountain inn is located at the hot sulfur springs that are said to be the Fountain of Youth of Ponce de León's dreams. Rooms open onto latticed wooden verandas and have a pleasing blend of contemporary and period furnishings. All are air-conditioned and have private bath. The parador can make arrangements for you to ride Puerto Rico's glorious, unique *paso fino* horses. ⊠ *Box 540, 00769,* ☎ *787/825–2186 or 800/443–0266,* 𝐅𝐀𝐗 *787/825– 4739. 48 rooms. Restaurant, lounge, air-conditioning, pool, hot springs. AE, DC, MC, V. EP.*

Dorado

$$$$ ⊞ **Hyatt Dorado Beach.** The ambience is a bit more sub-
★ dued at this resort than at its sister, the Cerromar Beach (☞ *below*), and guests can take advantage of the facilities there. A variety of elegant accommodations are in low-rise buildings scattered over 1,000 lavishly landscaped acres— among the most beautiful in the Caribbean. Most rooms have private patios or balconies, and all have polished terra-cotta floors, marble baths, and air-conditioning. Upper-level rooms in the Oceanview Houses have a view of the two half-moon beaches. ⊠ *Rte. 693, 00646,* ☎ *787/796–1234 or 800/233–1234,* 𝐅𝐀𝐗 *787/796–2022. 298 rooms. 3 restaurants, 2 lounges, air-conditioning, 2 pools, wading pool, spa, 2 18-hole Robert Trent Jones golf courses, 7 tennis courts, health club, hiking, jogging, water-sports center, bicycles, casino. AE, DC, MC, V. EP, MAP.*

$$$$ ⚄ **Hyatt Regency Cerromar Beach.** One of the best sports-oriented resorts in the Caribbean, the family-oriented Cerromar has two Robert Trent Jones golf courses, 14 tennis courts, a spa and health club, jogging and biking trails, a 900-foot river pool, a Jacuzzi in a man-made cavern, a swim-up bar, and a three-story-high water slide. It's 22 miles west of San Juan, right on the Atlantic. The modern seven-story hotel is done up in tropical style. Rooms have tile floors, marble baths, air-conditioning, and a king-size or two double beds. You'll find quieter rooms on the west side, away from the pool activity. Guests at the Cerromar and its sister facility, the Hyatt Dorado Beach (☞ *above*) a mile down the road, have access to the facilities of both resorts, and colorful red trolleys make frequent runs between the two. Sushi Wong's serves delicious pan-Asian cuisine, and Medici's is a sophisticated northern Italian eatery. ⊠ *Rte. 693, Km 11.8, 00646,* ☎ *787/796–1234 or 800/233–1234,* FAX *787/796–4647. 506 rooms. 3 restaurants, 3 bars, sushi bar, air-conditioning, pool, spa, 2 18-hole Robert Trent Jones golf courses, 14 tennis courts, health club, hiking, jogging, bicycles, casino with live entertainment, dance club. AE, DC, MC, V. EP, MAP.*

Guánica

$$$ ⚄ **Copamarina Beach Resort.** Sprawling across 18 acres be-
★ tween the sea and the Guánica Dry Forest is this quiet, landscaped resort. The pool is the centerpiece of the property, surrounded by the open-air reception area, manicured lawns, the outdoor Las Palmas Cafe, the elegant Ballena restaurant and bar, and the building wings. The bay bottom on this section of beach is covered in seaweed, but secluded beaches with clear water can be found a few minutes' drive down the road. The spotless rooms have small terraces with water views, one queen-size or two double beds, TV, phone, and air-conditioning. The furniture is bleached-wood-and-rattan, and the bedspreads are the ubiquitous tropical print. Try the red snapper in the dining room, and stop in the bar for the bartender's straight-up margarita. Arrange a snorkeling excursion to Gilligan's Island, an offshore key. Kayaks, sailboats, paddleboats, and tennis rackets are some of the gear for rent. There are plans to add 55 rooms, 15 villas, and a convention center to the complex.

Rte. 333, Km 6.5, Caña Gorda, Guánica, Box 805,
00653, ☎ 787/821–0505 or 800/468–4553, FAX 787/821–
0070. 70 rooms. 2 restaurants, 2 bars, air-conditioning, 2
pools, hot tub, 2 tennis courts, volleyball, scuba-diving
packages, bicycles, gift shop, recreation room, meeting
rooms. AE, D, DC, MC, V. EP.

Humacao

$$$–$$$$
★
🏨 **Palmas del Mar.** This luxurious resort community is on
2,750 acres of a former coconut plantation on the sheltered
southeast coast (about an hour's drive from San Juan).
Two hotels, the 23-suite Palmas Inn and 100-room Can-
delero Hotel, are the centerpieces of the complex. In the
rustic yet elegant Candelero, rooms are airy and spacious.
Ask for a room on the third floor, where there are cathe-
dral ceilings. The Palmas Inn suites, all with stunning sea
or garden views, evoke luxurious Mediterranean villas,
with pastel-pink connecting walkways, cobblestone plazas,
and fountains adorned with hand-painted tile work. The
resort includes private homes and condominium villas.
✉ Box 2020, Rte. 906, 00792, ☎ 787/852–6000 or 800/
468–3331, FAX 787/852–6330. 100 rooms; 140 villas; 23
1-, 2-, and 3-bedroom suites. 10 restaurants, air-condi-
tioning, pool, 18-hole Gary Player golf course, 20 tennis
courts, equestrian center, exercise room, beach, sailing,
scuba diving, marina, water-sports center, fishing, bicy-
cles, casino. AE, DC, MC, V. EP, MAP.

Jayuya

$
★
🏨 **Parador Hacienda Gripiñas.** Don't stay here if you're look-
ing for a beach vacation: The sea is more than 30 miles away.
This white hacienda is for those looking for a romantic
mountain hideaway. Polished wood and beam ceilings
warm the interior. Large airy rooms are decorated with na-
tive crafts. Relaxation beckons at every turn: Rocking
chairs nod in the spacious lounge, hammocks swing on the
porch, and splendid gardens invite a leisurely stroll. Your
morning coffee is grown on the adjacent working planta-
tion, and its aroma seems to fill the grounds, as does the
chirp of the ubiquitous coquis (tree frogs). ✉ Rte. 527, Km
2.5, Box 387, 00664, ☎ 787/828–1717 or 800/443–
0266, FAX 787/721–4698. 19 rooms. Restaurant, lounge,
pool, hiking. AE. EP.

La Parguera

$$ **Parador Villa Parguera.** This parador is a stylish hotel
★ on Phosphorescent Bay. Large, colorfully decorated rooms
have TV, phone, air-conditioning, private bath, and balcony
or terrace. A spacious dining room, overlooking the small
swimming pool and the bay beyond, serves excellent native and international dishes. Children under 10 stay free
in their parents' room. Ask about honeymoon packages.
✉ *Rte. 304, Box 273, Lajas 00667,* ☎ *787/899–3975 or
800/443–0266,* 𝐅𝐀𝐗 *787/899–6040. 62 rooms. Restaurant,
lounge, air-conditioning, saltwater pool, nightclub. AE,
D, DC, MC, V. EP.*

Las Croabas

$$$$ 🏨 **El Conquistador Resort and Country Club.** This massive
★ $250 million complex is a world unto itself, divided into five
self-contained hotels. It's perched dramatically atop a 300-
foot bluff overlooking the Caribbean, the Atlantic, and the
El Yunque rain forest. The architecture is a harmonious blend
of Moorish and Spanish colonial: cobblestone streets, white
stucco and terra-cotta buildings, open-air plazas with soaring arches and tinkling fountains, tiled benches, and gas
lamps. Plants and colorful caged parrots decorate many of
the open spaces. One of the five hotels, Las Olas, is actually built into the cliff face. In all of the hotels, the stylish,
elegant decor in the large rooms runs toward the ubiquitous Caribbean rattan and pastels, spiced with native artwork. Each room has a seating area with couch, glass-top
coffee table, desk, chairs, and entertainment center. Enormous bathrooms have a sunken tub, long marble countertop, makeup mirror, and walk-in closet. Nice extras include
dimmer switches on bedside lamps, well-stocked minibars,
CD players, and VCRs. The hotel's beach is an offshore island, which you reach via shuttle boat. The pampering begins at LMM International Airport: The resort is the only
one on the island to operate a private lounge and provide
deluxe motor-coach transfers. The ride is a little over an hour.
✉ *Av. El Conquistador, Box 70001, Las Croabas 00738,*
☎ *787/863–1000 or 800/468–5228,* 𝐅𝐀𝐗 *787/863–6586.
918 rooms and suites. 10 restaurants, 3 bars, lounge, air-
conditioning, minibars, in-room VCRs, 5 pools, spa, 18-hole
Arthur Hills golf course, 7 tennis courts, health club, 32-*

slip marina, scuba diving, water-sports center, fishing, shops, casino, nightclub, children's program, business services, convention center, car rental. AE, D, DC, MC, V. EP.

Mayagüez

$$$–$$$$ ★ 🏨 **Mayagüez Hilton and Casino.** Built on 20 acres about 2 miles north of the city of Mayagüez, this pink stucco resort on the island's west coast is about a 2½-hour drive from San Juan. The superb Rotisserie restaurant is known for its lavish theme buffets and top-notch steaks and seafood. Rooms are air-conditioned and have minibar, TV, and telephone. The decor is typical tan-and-muted-pastel. Many rooms overlook the parking lot, although poolside rooms view the tropical gardens and Mayagüez harbor in the distance. The hotel caters mainly to businesspeople. ⊠ *Rte. 2, Km 152.5, Box 3629, 00681,* ☎ *787/831–7575 or 800/ 445–8667; in Puerto Rico, 800/462–3954;* FAX *787/265– 3020. 141 rooms, 3 suites, 10 junior suites. Restaurant, lounge, bar, air-conditioning, minibars, no-smoking rooms, Olympic-size pool, baby pool, hot tub, 3 tennis courts, exercise room, casino, dance club, playground, meeting rooms. AE, D, DC, MC, V. EP.*

Ponce

$$–$$$$ 🏨 **Ponce Hilton and Casino.** By far the biggest resort on the south coast, this cream-and-turquoise hotel, nestled amid 80 acres of landscaped gardens, caters to a corporate clientele. Completely self-contained, it offers three restaurants (La Hacienda's antiques mimic an old coffee plantation; the romantic and elegant La Cava has a working wine cellar and can be reserved for a private dinner), access to a public beach, casino, shopping arcade, pool, four tennis courts, a driving range, and a disco with pool tables and live music on weekends. Although the lobby has all the warmth of an airline terminal, the large guest rooms are attractive enough, decorated in sky blue, teal, and peach, and furnished with modern rattan. All have a minibar, safe, TV, phone, and balcony. The views are best from the fourth-floor rooms. A drawback is the hotel's location—a 10-minute cab ride from town. ⊠ *Rte. 14, Av. Santiago de los Caballeros, Box 7419, 00732,* ☎ *787/259–7676 or 800/445–8667,* FAX *787/259–7674. 156 rooms, 8 suites. 3 restaurants, 2 bars, in-room safes, minibars, pool, beauty salon, hot tub, driving*

range, 4 tennis courts, basketball, exercise room, Ping-Pong, volleyball, shops, casino, dance club, baby-sitting, business services, meeting rooms. AE, D, DC, MC, V. EP.

$-$$ 🏨 **Hotel Melia.** Set in the heart of Ponce and facing the Parque de Bombas and the Ponce Cathedral, this family-owned
★   hotel provides a wonderful, low-key base for exploring the marvelous turn-of-the-century architecture, museums, and landmarks of downtown Ponce. The lobby has an old-world feel, with high ceilings, tiled floors, and well-worn but charming decor (the plastic covers on the lobby lamp shades need to go, however). Rooms have standard, if somewhat dated, decor and have TVs, phones, and air-conditioning. Some of the rooms have balconies that overlook the park. Breakfast is served on the rooftop terrace, which offers pretty views of the city and mountains. ⊠ *2 Calle Cristina, Box 1431, 00733,* ☎ *787/842–0260,* 𝖥𝖠𝖷 *787/841–3602. 80 rooms. Restaurant, bar, air-conditioning. AE, MC, V. CP.*

Rincón

$$$$ 🏨 **Horned Dorset Primavera.** The emphasis here is on privacy and relaxation. The Spanish neocolonial-style resort
★   is tucked away amid lush landscaping overlooking the sea. The only sounds that you're likely to hear as you lounge on the long, secluded, narrow beach, are the crash of the surf and an occasional squawk from Pompidou, the enormous parrot in the lounge. Suites have private balconies and are exquisitely furnished with antiques, including handsome mahogany four-poster beds, dressers, and nightstands. Casa Escondido, opened in 1995, has eight rooms—some have their own plunge pool—and is designed as a typical turn-of-the-century Puerto Rican hacienda, with tile or wood floors, stately mahogany furnishings, private terraces, and black marble baths. There are no radios, televisions, or telephones in any of the resort's rooms. The elegant restaurant serves Continental cuisine in surroundings befitting royalty. A delightful Continental breakfast is served in the open-air lounge. The hotel is a member of the prestigious Relais & Châteaux group. Children under 12 are not permitted. ⊠ *Rte. 429, Km 3, Box 1132, 00743,* ☎ *787/823–4030 or 787/823–4050,* 𝖥𝖠𝖷 *787/823–5580. 30 rooms. Restaurant, lounge, pool, library. AE, MC, V. EP.*

$$ ⊞ **Lemontree Waterfront Cottages.** These sparkling, large
★ apartments sit right on the beach, with staircases from
their decks to the sand. There are four units, each with a
fully equipped kitchen, TV, telephone, and large deck with
mahogany-topped wet bar and gas grill. The owner-man-
agers, Mary Jeanne and Paul Hellings, have put their per-
sonal touches on the apartments. Paul creates all the detailed
woodwork, and Mary Jeanne designs the interiors. The
bright tropical decor includes local artwork on the walls.
There is one three-bedroom unit with two baths, one two-
bedroom unit, and two newer one-bedroom units. The
one-bedroom units have wooden cathedral ceilings and
picture windows. The beach is small, but larger ones are
close by. It's a 10-minute drive to downtown Rincón. ⊠
Rte. 429, Box 200, Rincón, ☎ *787/823–6452,* FAX *787/823–
5821. 4 units. Kitchens, beach, weekly maid service, laun-
dry service, linens provided. AE, MC, V.*

San Germán

$ ⊞ **Parador Oasis.** The Oasis, not far from the town's two
★ plazas, was a family mansion 200 years ago; the lobby re-
tains a taste of the house's history with peppermint-pink
walls and white-wicker furniture. The older rooms are
convenient—right off the lobby—but show their age. The
newer rooms in the rear lack character but are functional,
clean, and a little roomier. All have TV, phone, and air-con-
ditioning. ⊠ *72 Calle Luna, Box 144, 00683,* ☎ *787/892–
1100 or 800/443–0266,* FAX *787/892–1175. 52 rooms.
Restaurant, lounge, air-conditioning, pool, hot tub, sauna,
exercise room. AE, D, DC, MC, V. EP.*

Vieques

$$$ ⊞ **Inn on the Blue Horizon.** Known for its restaurant, Cafe
★ Blu, and its octagonal Blu bar, this small hotel sits on 20
windswept acres fronting the Caribbean. There are only three
rooms, but at press time, owners and former New Yorkers
James Weis and Billy Knight had plans to add more. Furnished with antiques, the rooms are sumptuous and lovely,
as is the patio/lounge area. ⊠ *Rte. 996, Box 1556, 00765,*
☎ *787/741–3318. 3 rooms. Restaurant, bar, pool. AE,
MC, V. CP.*

$$–$$$ ⊞ **Casa del Francés.** Self-professed curmudgeon Irving Green-
★ blatt, a former Bostonian, runs this atmospheric if somewhat

run-down guest house in a restored French sugar plantation great house. Rooms are rather plain but enormous, with vaulted 17-foot ceilings. The food is good, the pool inviting, the guests an eclectic mix, and Irving a true character who will regale you with horror stories of running a Caribbean hotel. The sightseeing boat for the phosphorescent bay leaves from here. ⊠ *Box 458, Esperanza 00765,* ☎ *787/741–3751,* ⒻⒶⓍ *787/741–2330. 18 rooms. Restaurant, bar, pool, snorkeling. AE, MC, V. EP, MAP (compulsory in season).*

$$–$$$
★
🏨 **Hacienda Tamarindo.** Set on a windswept hill with sweeping views of the Caribbean, the new Hacienda Tamarindo is the nicest place to stay on Vieques. Owners Burr and Linda Vail left Vermont to build this extraordinary small hotel—with a huge tamarind tree right in the middle! The rooms are all individually decorated but share excellent craftsmanship, like mahogany louvered doors, terra-cotta tiled floors, and custom-tiled baths. Some of the rooms have private terraces and hot tubs, and two are accessible to people with disabilities. Half of the rooms have air-conditioning, while the rest face the trade winds. All are furnished with an eclectic mix of art and antiques shipped from Vermont. A full American breakfast is served on the second-floor terrace. Guests can walk down the hill to the Inn on the Blue Horizon (☞ *above*) for lunch and dinner. Box lunches are available on request. Children under 12 are not permitted. ⊠ *Rte. 996, Box 1569, 00765,* ☎ *787/741–8525,* ⒻⒶⓍ *787/741–8525. 16 rooms. Honor bar, pool. AE, MC, V. FAP.*

$$
★
🏨 **Crow's Nest.** Owner Liz O'Dell has made her simple but comfortable inn a very satisfying place to stay on Vieques. A Southerner by way of Massachusetts, Liz is a wealth of information and hospitality. She will arrange for you to do just about anything that's available on the island. Her 13-room lodging, set on 5 hilltop acres with pretty ocean views, is a great value. All rooms have kitchenettes and most are air-conditioned. Liz provides beach chairs and coolers for guests—a thoughtful touch. There is a lounge with TV/VCR, and one of the island's best restaurants, also called the Crow's Nest, is on the premises. ⊠ *Rte. 201, Km 1.6, Box 1521, 00765,* ☎ *787/741–0033,* ⒻⒶⓍ *787/741–1294. 13 rooms. Restaurant, bar, kitchenettes, pool, car rental. AE, MC, V. EP.*

Villa and Apartment Rentals

Villa and condominium or apartment rentals are becoming increasingly popular in Puerto Rico, particularly outside San Juan. If you are traveling with several people, these are often a very affordable option. Call the tourist information office in the area where you are interested in staying, or try the options listed below.

If you're part of a large group or you'd like to investigate off-season rates at higher-end properties in the Isla Verde area of San Juan, contact **Condo World** (⊠ 26645 W. Twelve Mile Rd., Southfield, MI 48034, ☎ 800/521–2980). For rentals out on the island, try **Island West Properties** (⊠ Rte. 413, Km 1.3, Box 700, Rincón 00677, ☎ 787/823–2323, 𝔽𝔸𝕏 787/823–3254). It has weekly and monthly vacation rentals that fall into the **$** to **$$** range. For rentals on Vieques, the person to talk to is Jane Sabin at **Connections** (⊠ Box 358, Vieques, 00765, ☎ 787/741–0023 or 800/772–3050). Or try **Acacia Apartments** (⊠ 236 Calle Acacia, Esperanza, Vieques, 00765, ☎ 787/741–1856).

5 Nightlife

HE OFFICIAL VISITORS' GUIDE, *¿Qué Pasa?,* has current listings of events in San Juan and out on the island. Also, pick up a copy of the *San Juan Star, Quick City Guide,* or *Sunspots,* and check with the local tourist offices and the concierge at your hotel to find out what's doing.

Fridays and Saturdays are big nights in San Juan. Dress to party. Bars are usually always casual. However, if you try to go out in jeans, sneakers, and a T-shirt, you will probably be refused entry at most nightclubs or discos (except the gay ones), unless you look like a model.

Bars

Calle San Sebastián in Old San Juan is lined with trendy bars and restaurants; if you're in the mood for barhopping, head in that direction—it's pretty crazy on weekend nights.

Blue Dolphin (⊠ 2 Calle Amapola, Isla Verde, ☎ 787/791–3083) is a hangout where you can rub elbows with some offbeat locals and enjoy some stunning sunset happy hours. While strolling along the Isla Verde beach, just look for the neon blue dolphin on the roof—you can't miss it. **El Patio de Sam** (⊠ 102 Calle san Sebastián, Old San Juan, ☎ 787/723–1149) is an Old San Juan institution whose expatriate clientele claims it serves the best burgers on the island. The dining room is awash in potted plants and strategically placed canopies that create the illusion of dining on an outdoor patio. **Hard Rock Cafe** (⊠ 253 Recinto Sur, Old San Juan, ☎ 787/724–7625), almost as common as McDonald's these days, is in Old San Juan.

Casinos

By law, all casinos are in hotels, primarily in San Juan. The government keeps a close eye on them. Dress for the larger casinos tends to be on the more formal side, and the atmosphere is refined. The law permits casinos to operate noon–4 AM, but individual casinos set their own hours.

Casinos are located in the following San Juan hotels (☞ Chapter 4): **Condado Plaza Hotel, Caribe Hilton, Dutch Inn & Tower** (⊠ 999 Ashford Ave., Condado), **Sands, El San Juan, Holiday Inn Crowne Plaza** (⊠ Rte. 187, Isla Verde), and **Radisson Ambassador** (⊠ 1369 Ashford Ave., Condado). Elsewhere on the island, there are casinos at the **Hyatt Regency Cerromar** and **Hyatt Dorado Beach** hotels, and at **Palmas del Mar,** the **Ponce Hilton,** the **El Conquistador,** and the **Mayagüez Hilton.**

Discos

Out on the island nightlife is hard to come by, but there are discos in the **Mayagüez** and **Ponce Hiltons.**

Amadeus (⊠ El San Juan Hotel, Isla Verde, ☎ 787/791– 1000) is a flashy disco in Isla Verde that attracts a well-dressed local crowd who come here to impress their dates and shake it. **Club Ibiza** (⊠ La Concha Hotel, ☎ 787/721– 6090) is the hot spot on Fridays, with an interesting, mixed crowd. At press time, the former site of the now-defunct Peggy Sue was being transformed into a new, glamorous club to be called **Egypt** (⊠ Robert Todd Ave., San Juan, ☎ 787/725–4664 or 787/725–4675). **Krash** (⊠ 1257 Av. Ponce de León, Santurce, ☎ 787/722–1390) plays the best dance music on the island; gay crowds flock here. **Lazers** (⊠ 251 Calle Cruz, ☎ 787/721–4479), with multilevels and a landscaped roof deck overlooking San Juan, attracts different crowds on different nights; Thursdays and Sundays are gay nights.

Festivals

LeLoLai is a year-round festival that celebrates Puerto Rico's Indian, Spanish, and African heritage. Performances take place each week, moving from hotel to hotel, showcasing the island's music, folklore, and culture. Because it is sponsored by the Puerto Rico Tourism Company and major San Juan hotels, passes to the festivities are included in some packages offered by participating hotels. You can also purchase tickets to a weekly series of events for $10. Contact the El Centro Convention Center, 787/723–3135. Reservations can be made by telephoning 787/722–1513. **La Tasca del Callejon** (⊠ Calle Fortaleza 317, ☎ 787/721–1689) is renowned for its tapas bar and the cabaret show (usually including flamenco guitar) performed by its engaging, talented staff.

Nightclubs

The Sands Hotel's **Players Lounge** brings in such big names as Joan Rivers, Jay Leno, and Rita Moreno. Try El San Juan's **El Chico** to dance to Latin music in a western saloon setting. The Condado Plaza Hotel's **La Fiesta Lounge** sizzles with steamy Latin shows. The **Casino Lounge** offers live jazz Wednesday through Saturday. The El Centro Convention Center offers the festive **Olé Latino** Latin revue (☎ 787/722–8433). **Houlihan's** (⊠ Ashford and Condado Aves., Condado, ☎ 787/723–8600) is a restaurant with an upstairs nightclub popular among the local party crowd. On weekends there is always a line of revelers on the sidewalk waiting to get in.

6 Outdoor Activities, Sports, and Beaches

OUTDOOR ACTIVITIES AND SPORTS

Baseball

THE ISLAND'S SEASON RUNS October–February. Many major-league ballplayers in the United States got their start in Puerto Rico's baseball league, and some return in the off-season to hone their skills. Stadiums are in San Juan, Santurce, Ponce, Caguas, Arecibo, and Mayagüez; the teams also play once or twice in Aguadilla. Contact the tourist office for details or call **Professional Baseball of Puerto Rico** (☎ 787/765–6285).

Bicycling

The broad beach at Boquerón makes for easy wheeling. You can rent bikes at **Boquerón Balnearios** (✉ Rte. 101, Boquerón, Dept. of Recreation and Sports, ☎ 787/722–1551 or 787/722–1771). In the Dorado area on the north coast, bikes can be rented at the **Hyatt Regency Cerromar Beach** (☎ 787/796–1234) or the **Hyatt Dorado Beach** (☎ 787/796–1234). Bikes are for rent at many of the hotels out on the island, including the **Ponce Hilton** (☎ 787/259–7676) and the **Copamarina Beach Resort** (☎ 787/821–0505).

Boating

Virtually all the resort hotels on San Juan's Condado and Isla Verda strips rent paddleboats, Sunfish, Windsurfers, kayaks, and the like. Contact **Condado Plaza Hotel Watersports Center** (☎ 787/721–1000, ext. 1361), the **El San Juan Hotel Watersports Center** (☎ 787/791–1000), or the **Caribe Hilton** (☎ 787/721–0303). Out on the island, your hotel will be able either to provide rentals or recommend rental outfitters.

Fishing

Half-day, full-day, split charters, and big- and small-game fishing can be arranged through **Benitez Deep-Sea Fishing** (⊠ Club Náutico de San Juan, Miramar, ☎ 787/723–2292), **Castillo Watersports** (⊠ ESJ Towers, Isla Verde, ☎ 787/791–6195 or 787/726–5752), and **Caribe Aquatic Adventures** (⊠ Radisson Normandie, ☎ 787/724–1882, ext. 240). Out on the island, try **Tropical Fishing Charters** (⊠ El Conquistador, Fajardo, ☎ 787/863–1000 or 787/789–5564), **Dorado Marine Center** (⊠ 271 Méndez Vigo, ☎ 787/796–4645), and **Parguera Fishing Charters** (⊠ Lajas, ☎ 787/899–4698 or 787/382–4698).

Fitness

While most hotels and resorts have some semblance of a gym for the buff-body crazed, three gyms in San Juan stand out for their superb equipment: **Le Spa Fitness Center** (⊠ San Juan Marriott, ☎ 787/722–7000), **Muscle Factory** (⊠ 1302 Ave. Ashford, ☎ 787/721–0717), and **Fitness City** (⊠ 1959 Calle Loiza, Suite 401, Ocean Park, ☎ 787/268–7773).

Golf

There are four beautiful Robert Trent Jones–designed 18-hole courses shared by the **Hyatt Dorado Beach** and the **Hyatt Regency Cerromar Beach** hotels (⊠ Dorado, ☎ 787/796–1234, ext. 3238 or 3016). You'll also find 18-hole courses at the **Palmas del Mar resort** (⊠ Humacao, ☎ 787/852–6000), the **Berwind Country Club** (⊠ Río Grande, ☎ 787/876–3056), **Club Ríomar** (⊠ Río Grande, ☎ 787/887–3964), the **El Conquistador** (⊠ Fajardo, ☎ 787/863–1000, hotel guests only), and **Punta Borinquén** (⊠ Aguadilla, ☎ 787/890–2987). The **Bahia Beach Plantation** (⊠ Río Grande, ☎ 787/256–5600) is Puerto Rico's newest course. There are two 9-hole courses out on the island, one at the **Club Deportivo del Oeste** (⊠ Cabo Rojo, ☎ 787/851–8880), and one at the **Aguirre Golf Club** (⊠ Aguirre, ☎ 787/853–4052). The **Ponce Hilton** (⊠ Ponce, ☎ 787/259–7676) has a driving range. Be sure to call ahead when you

n to play; public hours at these courses vary, and you
should schedule a tee time.

Hiking

Dozens of trails lace **El Yunque** (information is available at
the Sierra Palm Visitor Center, Rte. 191, Km 11.6, ☎ 787/
887–2875 or 787/766–5335). You can also hit the trails
in **Río Abajo Forest** (south of Arecibo) and **Toro Negro Forest** (east of Adjuntas). Each reserve has a ranger station.

Horse Racing

Thoroughbred races are run year-round at **El Comandante
Racetrack.** On race days the dining rooms open at 12:30
PM. ✉ *Rte. 3, Km 15.3, Canóvanas,* ☎ *787/724–6060.* ☉
Wed., Fri., Sun., holidays 12:30–6.

Horseback Riding

Beach trail rides can be arranged at **Palmas del Mar Equestrian Center** (✉ Palmas del Mar, Humacao, ☎ 787/852–
6000). **Hacienda Carabalí** (✉ Rte. 992, Km 4, Luquillo,
☎ 787/889–5820) offers beach riding and rain-forest trail
rides.

Sailing

Sailing instruction is offered by **Palmas Sailing Center** (✉
Palmas del Mar, Humacao, ☎ 787/852–6000, ext. 10310)
and most of the large resort hotels. Trips are offered by **Caribe
Aquatic Adventures** (✉ Radisson Normandie, ☎ 787/729–
2929, ext. 240) and **Castillo Watersports** (✉ ESJ Towers,
Isla Verde, ☎ 787/791–6195 or 787/726–5752). Rentals
are available at many hotels around the island.

Snorkeling and Scuba Diving

There is excellent diving off Puerto Rico's coast. Some outfits offer package deals combining accommodations with
daily diving trips; check when making your arrangements.
Escorted half-day dives range from $45 to $90 for one- and
two-tank dives, including all equipment. Packages, which

include lunch and other extras, start at $60. Night dives are often available at close to double the price. Snorkeling excursions, which include equipment rental and sometimes lunch, start at $25. Snorkel equipment rents at beaches for about $5.

Caution: Coral-reef waters and mangrove areas can be dangerous to novices. Unless you're an expert or have an experienced guide, avoid unsupervised areas and stick to the water-sports centers of major hotels.

Snorkeling and scuba-diving instruction and equipment rentals are available at **Boquerón Dive Shop** (⊠ Main St., Boquerón, ☎ 787/851–2155), **Caribbean School of Aquatics** (⊠ Taft #1, Suite 10F, San Juan, ☎ 787/728–6606), **Caribe Aquatic Adventures** (⊠ Radisson Normandie, ☎ 787/729–2929, ext. 240), **Coral Head Divers** (⊠ Palmas del Mar, Humacao, ☎ 787/852–6000 or 800/468–3331), **Dive Copamarina** (⊠ Copamarina Beach Resort, R. 333, Guánica, ☎ 787/821–6009; hotel-dive packages available), **Island Queen** (⊠ Rincón, ☎ 787/823–6301), **Parguera Divers Training Center** (⊠ La Parguera, ☎ 787/899–4171), and **Viking Puerto Rico** (⊠ Rincón, ☎ 787/823–7010).

Surfing

The best surfing beaches are along the Atlantic coastline from Borinquén Point south to Rincón, where there are several surf shops. Surfing is best from November through April. Aviones and La Concha beaches in San Juan and Casa de Pesca in Arecibo are summer surfing spots and have nearby surf shops.

Tennis

If you'd like to use the courts at a property where you are not a guest, call in advance for information about reservations and fees.

There are 17 lighted courts at **San Juan Central Park** (⊠ Calle Cerra exit on Rte. 2, ☎ 787/722–1646); 6 lighted courts at the **Caribe Hilton Hotel** (⊠ Puerta de Tierra, ☎ 787/721–0303, ext. 1730); 8 courts, 4 lighted, at **Carib Inn**

(⊠ Isla Verde, ☎ 787/791–3535, ext. 6); and 2 lighted courts at the **Condado Plaza Hotel** (⊠ Condado, ☎ 787/721–1000, ext. 1775). Out on the island, there are 14 courts, 2 lighted, at **Hyatt Regency Cerromar Beach** (⊠ Dorado, ☎ 787/796–1234, ext. 3040); 7 courts, 2 lighted, at the **Hyatt Dorado Beach** (⊠ Dorado, ☎ 787/796–1234, ext. 3220); 20 courts, 4 lighted, at **Palmas del Mar** (⊠ Humacao, ☎ 787/852–6000, ext. 51); 3 lighted courts (and a practice wall) at the **Mayagüez Hilton** (⊠ Mayagüez, ☎ 787/831–7575, ext. 2150); 4 lighted courts at the **Ponce Hilton** (⊠ Ponce, ☎ 787/259–7676); and 4 lighted courts at **Punta Borinquén** (⊠ Aguadilla, ☎ 787/891–8778).

Windsurfing

Many resort hotels rent Windsurfers to their guests, including the **El San Juan**, the **El Conquistador, Palmas del Mar,** the **Hyatts,** and the **Condado Plaza.** If your hotel doesn't provide them, they can probably help you make arrangements with a local outfitter.

BEACHES

By law, all of Puerto Rico's beaches are open to the public (except for the Caribe Hilton's man-made beach in San Juan). The government runs 13 *balnearios* (public beaches), which have dressing rooms, lifeguards, parking, and in some cases picnic tables, playgrounds, and camping facilities. Admission is free, parking $1. Most balnearios are open 9–5 daily in summer and Tuesday through Sunday the rest of the year. Listed below are some major balnearios. You can also contact the Department of Recreation and Sports (☎ 787/722–1551 or 787/722–1771).

Boquerón Beach, on the southwest coast, is a broad beach of hard-packed sand fringed with coconut palms. It has picnic tables, cabin rentals, bike rentals, basketball court, minimarket, scuba diving, and snorkeling. **Isla Verde,** a white sandy beach bordered by huge resort hotels, offers picnic tables and good snorkeling, with equipment rentals nearby. Set near San Juan, it's a lively beach popular with city folk. **Luquillo Beach** is crescent-shaped and comes complete with coconut palms, picnic tables, and tent sites. Coral reefs protect its crystal-clear lagoon from the Atlantic waters, making it ideal for swimming. It's one of the largest and best-known beaches on the island, and it gets crowded on weekends. **Ocean Park,** a residential neighborhood just east of the Condado, is home to the prettiest beach in San Juan. Here you'll find a mile-long, wide stretch of fine golden sand and often choppy but very swimmable waters. Very popular on weekends with local college students, this is also one of the cities' two gay beaches (the other is in front of the Atlantic Beach Hotel). **Playa Flamenco,** one of the most beautiful beaches in the Caribbean, is on the north shore of Culebra. The 3-mile-long crescent has shade trees, picnic tables, and rest rooms. It is popular on weekends with day-trippers from Fajardo. During the winter, storms in the North Atlantic often create great waves for bodysurfing. **Playa Soni,** on the eastern end of Culebra, is a wide strand of sparkling white sand on a protected bay with calm waters. Views of the islets of Culebrita, Cayo Norte, and St. Thomas are stunning. As there are no facilities and little shade, bring lots of water and an umbrella. **Seven Seas Beach,** an elongated beach of hard-packed sand, is always popular with bathers. It has picnic tables and tent and trailer sites; snorkeling, scuba diving, and boat rentals are nearby. **Sun Bay,** a white-sand beach on the island of Vieques, has shade trees, picnic tables, and tent sites, and offers snorkeling and scuba diving. Boat rentals are nearby.

7 Shopping

SAN JUAN IS NOT A FREE PORT, and you won't find bargains on electronics and perfumes. You can, however, find excellent prices on china, crystal, fashions, and jewelry. Shopping for local Caribbean crafts can be great fun. You'll run across a lot of tacky things you can live without, but you can also find some treasures, and in many cases you'll be able to watch the artisans at work. (For guidance, contact the Puerto Rico Tourism Company's Artisan Center, ☎ 787/721–2400, ext. 2201, or the Fomento Crafts Project, ☎ 787/758–4747, ext. 2291.)

Shopping Districts

Old San Juan is full of shops, especially on Cristo, Fortaleza, and San Francisco streets. **Plaza Las Américas,** south of San Juan, is the largest shopping mall in the Caribbean, with 200 shops, restaurants, and movie theaters. Other malls out on the island include **Plaza del Caribe** in Ponce, **Plaza del Carmen** in Caguas, and the **Mayagüez Mall.**

Specialty Shops

Clothing

You can get discounts on Hathaway shirts and Christian Dior clothing at **Hathaway Factory Outlet** (⊠ 203 Calle Cristo, ☎ 787/723–8946). Discounts on Ralph Lauren apparel are found at the **Polo/Ralph Lauren Factory Store** (⊠ 201 Calle Cristo, ☎ 787/722–2136). The **London Fog Factory Outlet** (⊠ 156 Calle Cristo, ☎ 787/722–4334) offers reductions on men's, women's, and children's raincoats. People line up to enter **Marshalls** (⊠ Plaza de Armas, ☎ 787/722–0874) in Old San Juan. Try the **Bikini Factory** (⊠ 3 Palmar Norte, Isla Verde, ☎ 787/726–0016) for stylish men's and women's swimwear.

Jewelry

There is gold, gold, and more gold at **Reinhold** (⊠ 201 Calle Cristo, ☎ 787/725–6878). For brand-name watches visit the **Watch and Gem Palace** (⊠ 204 Calle San José, Old San Juan, ☎ 787/722–2136).

Local Crafts

For one-of-a-kind buys, head for **Puerto Rican Arts & Crafts** (⊠ 204 Calle Fortaleza, Old San Juan, ☎ 787/725–5596). You should pay a visit to the **artisan markets** in Sixto Escobar Park (⊠ Puerta de Tierra, ☎ 787/722–0369) and Luis Muñoz Marín Park (⊠ Next to Las Américas Expressway west on Piñero Ave., Hato Rey, ☎ 787/763–0568). The **Haitian Gallery** (⊠ 367 Calle Fortaleza, ☎ 787/725–0986) carries Puerto Rican crafts and a selection of folksy, often inexpensive paintings from around the Caribbean. In Ponce, consult the **Casa Paoli Center of Folkloric Investigations** (⊠ 14 Calle Mayor, ☎ 787/840–4115).

Paintings and Sculptures

Corinne Timsit International Galleries (⊠ 104 Calle San Jose, Old San Juan, ☎ 787/724–1039) features work by contemporary Latin American painters. **DMR Gallery** (⊠ 204 Calle Luna, Old San Juan, ☎ 787/722–4181) features handmade furniture by artist Nick Quijano. **Galería Botello** (⊠ 208 Calle Cristo, Old San Juan, ☎ 787/723–2879; ⊠ Plaza Las Américas, ☎ 787/754–7430) exhibits and sells antique santos (religious sculptures). **Galería Gotay** (⊠ 212 Calle San Francisco, Old San Juan, ☎ 787/722–5726) carries contemporary art in many medias. Another gallery worth visiting is the **Galería San Juan** (⊠ Gallery Inn, 204–206 Calle Norzagaray, Old San Juan, ☎ 787/722–1808), especially to view the sculptures of bronze artist Jan D'Esopo.

Gift Ideas

Popular souvenirs and gifts include *santos* (small, hand-carved figures of saints or religious scenes), hand-rolled cigars, handmade *mundillo* lace from Aguadilla, Carnival masks (papier-mâché from Ponce and fierce *veijigantes* made from coconut husks in Loiza, an African-American enclave near San Juan), and fancy men's shirts called *guayaberas*. Also, some folks swear that Puerto Rican rum is the best in the world.

It helps to be pushy in airports.

Introducing the revolutionary new TransPorter™ from American Tourister® It's the first suitcase you can push around without a fight. TransPorter's™ exclusive four-wheel design lets you push it in front of you with almost no effort–the wheels take the weight. Or pull it on two wheels if you choose. You can even stack on other bags and use it like a luggage cart.

Stable 4-wheel design.

TransPorter™ is designed like a dresser, with built-in shelves to organize your belongings. Or collapse the shelves and pack it like a traditional suitcase. Inside, there's a suiter feature to help keep suits and dresses from wrinkling. When push comes to shove, you can't beat a TransPorter™ For more information on how you can be this pushy, call 1-800-542-1300.

Shelves collapse on command.

American Tourister®

Making travel less primitive.®

©1996 American Tourister®

Your passport around the world.

- Worldwide access
- Operators who speak your language
- Monthly itemized billing

MCI Calling Card

415 555 1234 2244
J.D. SMITH

Use your MCI Card® and these access numbers for an easy way to call when traveling worldwide.

American Samoa	633-2MCI (633-2624)
Antigua†	#2
(Available from public card phones only)	
Aruba❖	800-888-8
Argentina★†	001-800-333-1111
Bahamas(CC)†	1-800-888-8000
Barbados	1-800-888-8000
Belize	815 from pay phones
	557 from hotels
Bermuda❖††	1-800-888-8000
Bolivia♦	0-800-2222
Brazil(CC)†	000-8012
British Virgin Islands❖	1-800-888-8000
Cayman Islands†	1-800-888-8000
Chile(CC)†	
To call using CTC■	800-207-300
To call using ENTEL■	123-00316
Colombia(CC)♦†	980-16-0001
Costa Rica♦†	0800-012-2222
Dominica	1-800-888-8000
Dominican Republic(CC)	1-800-888-8000
Ecuador(CC)❖†	999-170
El Salvador♦	800-1767
Grenada❖	1-800-888-8000

Guatemala♦	189
Guyana	177
Haiti(CC)❖	001-800-444-1234
Honduras❖	122
Jamaica	1-800-888-8000
(From Special Hotels only)	873
Mexico▲†	95-800-674-7000
Netherlands Antilles(CC)❖††	
	001-800-950-1022
Nicaragua(CC)	166
(Outside of Managua, dial 02 first)	
Panama†	108
Military Bases	2810-108
Paraguay❖	008-11-800
Peru	170
Puerto Rico(CC)†	1-800-888-8000
St. Lucia❖	1-800-888-8000
Trinidad & Tobago❖	1-800-888-8000
Turks & Caicos❖	1-800-888-8000
Uruguay	00-412
U.S. Virgin Islands(CC)†	1-800-888-8000
Venezuela❖†♦	800-1114-0

To sign up for the MCI Card, dial the access number of the country you are in and ask to speak with a customer service representative.

http://www.mci.com

8 Portrait of Puerto Rico

CITY OF LIGHT

THE LIGHT IS ALWAYS yellow in the morning streets. Even in the soft, drizzling rains of summer or the fierce, wind-driven storms of early fall, I feel bathed in that luminous yellow light. It seeps from the walls of the old houses—a light formed by the centuries, an antique light, a light that once held conquistadores and slaves, sugar kings and freebooters, the light of old gold and vanished supremacies—the light of San Juan.

When I say San Juan, I don't mean that great urban sprawl, with its population of more than a million, that makes up the modern capital of the island of Puerto Rico. That San Juan, with its office towers and traffic jams, raw concrete-block factories and heartless condominia, is just another city of the 20th century. When I think of San Juan, I mean the old town, called San Juan Antiguo by the formal, but more affectionately referred to as Viejo San Juan by those who know it and love it and have been warmed by its yellow light.

My San Juan, the old town I first saw in the late 1950s and have been visiting ever since, fills a mere seven square blocks on a promontory hooked around to face the great harbor that made the Spanish christen this island Rich Port. Across the centuries, it has been battered by unnamed tropical storms, and, in 1989, felt the power of Hurricane Hugo. But Viejo San Juan endures.

Whenever I visit Puerto Rico, arriving on a screaming jet at the airport in Isla Verde, I always go first to the old town. It centers me, in an island society that is too often culturally and politically schizophrenic. It grants me a sense of proportion. The modern city vanishes and much of the 20th century goes with it. Few places on this earth make me as happy.

The past is part of the reason. In many American cities now, we seem to be living in an eternal present tense, as insubstantial as the images on television screens. Too many events flash across our minds in unconnected fragments; today's crises are forgotten tomorrow; we hear too much and see too much and never listen for the whispering of ghosts. But there has been a San Juan since 1521, one hundred years before the first Dutchman mortared two bricks together to begin making New York. When the American Revolution began, San Juan had been there for 255 years.

So it is no accident that when I walk from Plaza Colón (with its statue of Columbus disguised as Dean Rusk) into Calle San Francisco, my sense of time shifts. The past asserts itself and I am reminded that for a long time before the rise of the United States this was a Spanish-speaking hemisphere. I hear the conversations of Puerto Ricans, delivered in the staccato-rhythms of port people, full of jokes and innuendo and untranslatable local words. The air is thick with vowels. From the old mortar of the walls, the past murmurs: Wait, slow down, listen, have a glass of rum, and remember old sins, the folly of man, the futility of despair.

Columbus discovered America in 1492, and on his second voyage the following year, the Admiral of the Ocean Sea landed at the site of the present town of Aguadilla on the northwest coast of the island. There were then about 30,000 Taino Indians living on the island, which they called Boringquén. There was little gold to plunder, and those first Spaniards quickly moved on. Their first settlement was established at Caparra in 1509, but was soon abandoned to the mosquitoes. The Spaniards moved out of the marshes to the promontory beside the great bay and began to build a town they called San Juan Bautista, for St. John the Baptist, who remains the island's patron saint. They built from memory, combining the Islamic clarity and the proportions of Andalusia with houses glimpsed in the Canary Islands before the passage across the fierce Atlantic. They used brick and the ax-breaking hardwood called *ausubo* as well as iron forged in their own shops. They built the place to last.

The city they made evolved over centuries, of course, and even today the urban archaeologists of the Institute of Puerto Rican Culture are trying to chart its transformations. This is no simple task. Although minibuses now move through the old town, and taxis can take you to some key points (other streets are blocked to cars), the best way to see San Juan is on foot.

As you walk the streets, you tread upon blue-slag bricks called *adoquines*. Some guides insist they were originally ballast in the sailing ships of the 17th and 18th centuries, dumped here as the ships took on cargoes of sugar and tobacco for the markets of Europe; others tell you they arrived in San Juan from England as late as 1890.

But they feel as if they had been here from the beginning, glistening with spring rain, perfect complements to the suffused yellow light.

Ni modo; it doesn't matter. They are part of San Juan forever. So is the feeling that here you might be safe. Three fortresses guard the city: La Fortalez—the oldest executive mansion in the hemisphere, now occupied by the island's governor—overlooking the bay on the southwest of the promontory; San Cristóbal, to the right as you enter the old town from the hotels of the Condado; the magnificent El Morro on the tip, its cannon pointing northwest into the Atlantic. Walls surround the city, linking the three great fortresses, walls of stone.

These walls and forts were not empty adornment; they were, like most things of beauty, a necessity. San Juan was established in an age of international gangsterism, and, since it was usually the last stop for Spanish galleons groaning with the loot of Mexico and Peru, hijackers saw it as an obvious target. Today, you can walk along the edge of El Morro, on walls that are 20 feet thick and rise 140 feet above the sea, and imagine what it was like when unfriendly sails on the horizon could mean death and destruction.

The fort was completed in 1589 by a team of military engineers headed by Juan Bautista Antonelli. The noted English gangster, Francis Drake, appeared in 1595 and was battered by the fort's six levels of cannons, along with fire from the smaller guns of La Fortaleza. Ten of Drake's ships were sunk, and more than 400 sailors were sent to the bottom of the harbor. But, three years later, another English hood, the Earl of Cumberland, arrived and came upon the city from the land side with a force of a thousand soldiers. He occupied San Juan, looted it, and then was forced to abandon it as more than 400 of his men perished from disease. El Morro never was captured again, although the Dutch tried in 1625, managing to burn a number of buildings in San Juan, including the finest private library then in existence in the New World. American naval gunners blasted away at the walls in 1898, during the war against Spain that made Puerto Rico an American colony. They never did take the fortress.

Today, you can visit El Morro on foot, with better luck than Cumberland's doomed soldiers. You go through the 27-acre park grounds, where soldiers once drilled and lovers now meet and fathers play ball with their sons. Hugo did its best against the park, damaging some 50 Australian pines that once lined its entrance. The National Park Service subsequently cut them down.

The hurricane also caused minor damage to the fort, but across the centuries it has survived well. Its walls are the color of lions, its arches painted white, and you cross a dry moat to enter the interior. From the ramparts, you can look down upon crashing surf, or you can visit the museum and souvenir shop, or examine the restored lighthouse, or photograph the domed sentry boxes called *garitas*. You can watch the pretty girls. Or you can simply surrender to the sense of time.

In the area of El Morro, I always save an hour to wander through the 19th century cemetery below the fortress walls; here lie many of the most famous Puerto Rican political leaders, the martyred revolutionaries, some of the old Spanish *peninsulares* (who lived lives of leisure while slaves did the work), and ordinary folk, too; shopkeepers and blacksmiths, shoemakers and chefs, and the artisans and craftsmen who built the town and died at home. Or I visit a while in La Casa Blanca, the oldest house on the island, built for Ponce de León in 1521. Ponce was a mixture of romantic and conqueror. He dreamed, as they all did in that generation of Spanish adventurers, of gold. In Puerto Rico, he found little of it—certainly nothing on the scale of the great treasures of Mexico. He stayed on for a while as governor, watching the Tainos die of European

diseases or flee to the jungle hills or depart down through the islands in great hand-hewn boats.

They were strange, those dark-skinned pagans; they simply would not agree to be slaves. So Ponce de León departed for Florida in search of the Fountain of Youth, almost certainly a fabrication invented by an Indian. Ponce was still searching in Florida when he was killed in a skirmish with Indians much fiercer than the Pacific Tainos. His body was first taken to Cuba, then to San Juan, and his bones are now in the Metropolitan Cathedral. But the elegant Casa Blanca remained in the Ponce family until the late 18th century. The town rose around them. Streets were laid out, fountains constructed, churches built. The energy of the first generation of conquistadores waned throughout the vast Spanish empire; adventurers were replaced with clerks and grandees. The family grew rich, was battered by history, and departed after 250 years. A series of Spanish and then American military commanders lived here, strutting around the lovely courtyard and the splashing fountains. The house is now occupied by the Institute for Advanced Studies.

As an object made by men, a collective work of sculpture, El Castillo de San Cristóbal is, to me, preferable to El Morro. You can walk to it along the city walls, looking down at La Perla, the most picturesque slum under the American flag (it was described in detail in anthropologist Oscar Lewis' book *La Vida*). In ordinary times, the green-tar-paper roofs of La Perla, and the flags of the island's political parties, stand precariously between the city walls and the sea. But Hugo blew the flags into eternity, ripped the tar paper from many rooftops, and battered some of the frailer structures. This was nothing new. Houses have been washed away by storms in the past, but the people of La Perla always come back and build again. Now, children run in the streets and winos flake out against the sides of houses. Years ago, I used to visit friends down here, but they don't live in La Perla anymore. And in the age of crack cocaine I no longer have the courage to wander its improvised streets.

Instead, I go to San Cristóbal, designed by two of those Irishmen known as the "wild geese"—the men and women who scattered around the world after the English conquest of their home island. Two who came to Puerto Rico were Alejandro O'Reilly and Thomas O'Daly, and, in the employ of the Spanish Army, they designed a fort laced with tunnels, secret traps, blind walls, gates, and pickets. The intention was to protect San Juan from land invasions, similar to Cumberland's. There are forts within forts here, like watertight compartments

in ships. An invader might take part of the fortress, but would pay a bloody and ferocious price to take it all.

I love the view from the ramparts of this fort, looking east toward the beaches and gigantic clouds that gather above the rain forest of the mountain called El Yunque. I like to think of O'Reilly and O'Daly, with their noses peeling, standing in the great blinding light of the summer sun, far from home, on a promontory cooled by the trade winds, speaking in Irish about one final go with the hated English.

Within the city's walls, there are streets that resemble those of New Orleans, with elaborately scrolled iron, balconies attached to three-story houses that loom imperiously above their smaller neighbors. Most were built in the 17th and 18th centuries by the hidalgos who grew rich from tobacco, sugar, and horses. The ceiling beams and front doors are cut from the ausubo tree, so hard that is has been known to make restoration workers cry. The austere walls are humanized by the bright colors of the Caribbean: lime green, aqua, cerulean blue, rose, and, of course, those warm ochres and yellows. In other places, such colors might seem garish; here, they are as natural and permanent as the sky and the sea.

But some things do change. When I first came to San Juan, there was always music coming from those scrolled balconies, through the open doors of apartments: The Trio Los Panchos and Tito Rodriguez, Augustin Lara and Lucho Gatica, music romantic and bittersweet, occasionally punctuated by the tougher rhythms of mambo. There is less music in the streets now because prosperity has brought air conditioning to Viejo San Juan, and, as everywhere in the world, air conditioning closes windows and doors.

But if there is less to hear, there is still much to see. You gaze into patios that are like snatches of Seville; small fountains, bird cages, polished-iron implements, flowers. All manner of flowers grow in elaborate terracotta pots: philodendron, orchids, the yellowing vines called canarios, bougainvillea spilling from balconies, and hibiscus—mounds, garlands, bowers of hibiscus. There is an occasional flamboyant tree, with its scarlet flowers, imprisoned in its city garden; or a flowering oleander or frangipani preening for the hibiscus. You see palm trees, too, those immigrants from Africa, with terns rattling in the fronds.

Most windows are shuttered, the mute houses implying that in the great Spanish centuries, the densest human life was lived behind them. The town was too small then, too bourgeois, too formal for public melodramas.

Today, life is more public. San Juan is not a museum, and as you wander the streets you can see old men playing dominoes in small, shaded squares, middle-aged women shopping in the boutiques or stopping in La Bombonera on Calle San Francisco for splendid coffee and oversweet pastries, and young people everywhere. I'm not much of a shopper; I'd rather look and imagine than own. So I ignore the shops and follow no set route on my wanderings through Viejo San Juan. I want to be reassured and surprised.

I always go to the Cristo Chapel on the city walls overlooking the harbor. Almost always it is as I saw it last, closed off by an iron gate, four potted palms within its small interior, the masonry peeled off parts of the walls to reveal the thin brick of the past. The palms were demolished by Hugo; they will be replaced. One need not share the belief that inspired the chapel to be charmed by its proportions and modesty. As always, the little park beside it is filled with children and pigeons. A plaque tells me that the chapel was built between 1753 and 1780 and that "legend traces its origin to a miraculous happening at the site." It doesn't describe the miracle, but it is said that in 1753 a rider in a holy festival made a mistake, plunged over the wall into the sea, and lived. Not exactly a major miracle, I suppose, but good enough to get the chapel built. The plaque bears the seal of Lions International.

As in most Latin countries, the sacred and the profane are at war here. All over Old San Juan, there are dozens of little bars. On the corner of San Sebastián and San Justo there is a bar called Aquí Se Puede, which means "here you can," and in its cool, dark interior the name seems more an act of reporting than of enticement.

A few blocks away is the Church of San José—spare, controlled, set facing a square out of deChirico. It is the oldest church still in active use in the Americas, built by Dominican friars in the 1530s. But the mood within is of an austere European Catholicism exiled to the tropics. Plain song comes from a hidden sound system. Natural light falls from openings in the cupolas of side chapels. The wooden pews are severe. The stations of the cross, with their ancient tale of sacrifice and pain, are bichromes of blue and white. Most afternoons, there is an eerie silence in the place, perhaps for good reason; archives suggest that as many as four thousand people—-including most of the descendants of Ponce de León— might be buried beneath the tile floors.

On hot days, I used to stop for a while in the Plaza de Armas, to sit under the shade trees and talk to the taxi drivers and lounging cops and gold-toothed old men. They all told fabulous lies, and, across the street, vendors sold flowers under the arches of City Hall. There were department stores on the harbor side and pretty girls everywhere. The stores and pretty girls remain; all the rest is changed.

In 1988, a mayor named Balthasar Corrado del Rió insisted on remodeling the plaza his way. Citizens protested, but he went ahead anyway—the shade trees were chain sawed at four in the morning. A cheap phone kiosk was erected. And now the Plaza de Armas is a bald, bright plain.

Now, if it's a hot day, I walk across the plaza to the corner of the New York Department Store, toward the harbor along Calle San José. I go into The Bookstore, which is air conditioned and has a fine selection of books in English, along with the latest volumes from Mexico, Buenos Aires, and Barcelona, and the works of such fine Puerto Rican writers as Pedro Juan Soto, Luis Rafael Sanchez, and Rene Marquez. Here I can also pick up a copy of *The New York Times*. Then I go next door into the Café de Los Amigos for the best coffee in the old town. A sign sets out one of the rules: *No Discuta Politica Aquí*.

There are other plazas, churches, and museums, of course; your legs will carry you to all of them, or, in revolt, will persuade you to see them at some later date. But the people are as important as the buildings. On Saturday nights, the young people of the other San Juan show up to party in Viejo San Juan; handsome young men in the pretty-boy *guapo* style—hair slicked wearing New York fashions, playing out roles that they haven't earned; the young women, voluptuous, made up to look like Madonna or one of the stars of Spanish television, their bodies bursting from tight skirts, T-shirts, and blouses.

There is something sad about them, as they preen for each other in the ancient rituals. They seem like so many tropical flowers bloomingly briefly before the swift move into adulthood. On these weekend evenings, they stand outside the Daiquiri Factory on Calle San Francisco, or Joseph's Café next door, some of them drinking and dancing inside while MTV plays on giant screens. They come to Viejo San Juan from the modern city of plastic and cement, as if subconsciously seeking to discover who they are by temporarily inhabiting the places from which their families came.

The perfumed rituals are enacted amidst the colliding symbols of the island's general cultural schizo-phrenia: Kentucky Fried Chicken, Burger King, and McDonald's, along with El Convento and the Plaza Salvador Brau, where there is a statue of a man named Patricio Rijos, who was known in life as "Toribio, King of the Guiro." The guiro is a grooved gourd played as a rhythm instrument with a wire fork. It is never seen on MTV.

And as the children of those San Juan nights career away to various appointments, the music gradually stops, doors are shuttered, the traffic departs. At 104 Calle Fortaleza, on one such evening, I stopped to look at a marble plaque that identified the building as: "THE HOUSE WHERE IN 1963 THE PIÑA COLADA WAS CREATED BY DON RAMON PORTA MINGOT." It was now a perfume shop called Barrachina. I smiled, thinking that in Viejo San Juan, all of the important things are remembered, when a small, wiry man came up to me.

"*Es una mentira,*" he said. "It's a lie. It was the bar of the Caribe Hilton, 1958."

Without another word, he walked off on unsteady legs, humming an old song. I went back to the hotel, to dream of yellow light.

— *By Pete Hamill*

SPANISH VOCABULARY

Words and Phrases

Basics

English	Spanish	Pronunciation
Yes/no	Sí/no	see/no
Please	Por favor	pore fah-vore
May I?	¿Me permite?	may pair-mee-tay
Thank you (very much)	(Muchas) gracias	(moo-chas) grah-see-as
You're welcome	De nada	day nah-dah
Excuse me	Con permiso	con pair-mee-so
Pardon me/what did you say?	¿Como?/¡Mánde?	ko-mo/mahn-dey
Could you tell me?	¿Podría decirme?	po-dree-ah deh-seer-meh
I'm sorry	Lo siento	lo see-en-toe
Good morning!	¡Buenos días!	bway-nohs dee-ahs
Good afternoon!	¡Buenas tardes!	bway-nahs tar-dess
Good evening!	¡Buenas noches!	bway-nahs no-chess
Goodbye!	¡Adiós!/¡Hasta luego!	ah-dee-ohss/ah-stah-lwe-go
Mr./Mrs.	Señor/Señora	sen-yor/sen-yore-ah
Miss	Señorita	sen-yo-ree-tah
Pleased to meet you	Mucho gusto	moo-cho goose-to
How are you?	¿Cómo está usted?	ko-mo es-tah oo-sted
Very well, thank you.	Muy bien, gracias.	moo-ee bee-en, grah-see-as
And you?	¿Y usted?	ee oos-ted
Hello (on the telephone)	Bueno	bwen-oh

Numbers

1	un, uno	oon, oo-no
2	dos	dos
3	tres	trace
4	cuatro	kwah-tro
5	cinco	sink-oh
6	seis	sace
7	siete	see-et-ey

8	ocho	o-cho
9	nueve	new-ev-ay
10	diez	dee-es
11	once	own-sey
12	doce	doe-sey
13	trece	tray-sey
14	catorce	kah-tor-sey
15	quince	keen-sey
16	dieciséis	dee-es-ee-sace
17	diecisiete	dee-es-ee-see-et-ay
18	dieciocho	dee-es-ee-o-cho
19	diecinueve	dee-es-ee-new-ev-ay
20	veinte	bain-tay
21	veinte y uno/veintiuno	bain-te-oo-no
30	treinta	train-tah
32	treinta y dos	train-tay-dose
40	cuarenta	kwah-ren-tah
43	cuarenta y tres	kwah-ren-tay-trace
50	cincuenta	seen-kwen-tah
54	cincuenta y cuatro	seen-kwen-tay kwah-tro
60	sesenta	sess-en-tah
65	sesenta y cinco	sess-en-tay seen-ko
70	setenta	set-en-tah
76	setenta y seis	set-en-tay sace
80	ochenta	oh-chen-tah
87	ochenta y siete	oh-chen-tay see-yet-ay
90	noventa	no-ven-tah
98	noventa y ocho	no-ven-tah o-cho
100	cien	see-en
101	ciento uno	see-en-toe oo-no
200	doscientos	doe-see-en-tohss
500	quinientos	keen-yen-tohss
700	setecientos	set-eh-see-en-tohss
900	novecientos	no-veh-see-en-tohss
1,000	mil	meel
2,000	dos mil	dose meel
1,000,000	un millón	oon meel-yohn

Colors

black	negro	*neh*-grow
blue	azul	ah-*sool*
brown	café	kah-*feh*
green	verde	*vair*-day
pink	rosa	*ro*-sah
purple	morado	mo-*rah*-doe
orange	naranja	na-*rahn*-hah
red	rojo	*roe*-hoe
white	blanco	*blahn*-koh
yellow	amarillo	ah-mah-*ree*-yoh

Days of the Week

Sunday	domingo	doe-*meen*-goh
Monday	lunes	*loo*-ness
Tuesday	martes	*mahr*-tess
Wednesday	miércoles	me-*air*-koh-less
Thursday	jueves	who-*ev*-ess
Friday	viernes	vee-*air*-ness
Saturday	sábado	*sah*-bah-doe

Months

January	enero	eh-*neh*-ro
February	febrero	feh-*brair*-oh
March	marzo	*mahr*-so
April	abril	ah-*breel*
May	mayo	*my*-oh
June	junio	*hoo*-nee-oh
July	julio	*who*-lee-yoh
August	agosto	ah-*ghost*-toe
September	septiembre	sep-tee-*em*-breh
October	octubre	oak-*too*-breh
November	noviembre	no-vee-*em*-breh
December	diciembre	dee-see-*em*-breh

Useful Phrases

Do you speak English?	¿Habla usted inglés?	*ah*-blah oos-*ted* in-*glehs*
I don't speak Spanish	No hablo español	no *ah*-blow es-pahn-*yol*
I don't understand (you)	No entiendo	no en-tee-*en*-doe
I understand (you)	Entiendo	en-tee-*en*-doe
I don't know	No sé	no *say*

I am American/ British	Soy americano(a)/ inglés(a)	soy ah-meh-ree-kah-no(ah)/ in-glace(ah)
What's your name?	¿Cómo se llama usted?	koh-mo say yah-mah oos-ted
My name is . . .	Me llamo . . .	may yah-moh
What time is it?	¿Qué hora es?	keh o-rah es
It is one, two, three . . . o'clock.	Es la una; son las dos, tres	es la oo-nah/sone lahs dose, trace
Yes, please/No, thank you	Sí, por favor/No, gracias	see pore fah-vor/no grah-see-us
How?	¿Cómo?	koh-mo
When?	¿Cuándo?	kwahn-doe
This/Next week	Esta semana/ la semana que entra	es-tah seh-mah-nah/lah say-mah-nah keh en-trah
This/Next month	Este mes/el próximo mes	es-tay mehs/el proke-see-mo mehs
This/Next year	Este año/el año que viene	es-tay ahn-yo/el ahn-yo keh vee-yen-ay
Yesterday/today/ tomorrow	Ayer/hoy/mañana	ah-yair/oy/mahn-yah-nah
This morning/ afternoon	Esta mañana/tarde	es-tah mahn-yah-nah/tar-day
Tonight	Esta noche	es-tah no-cheh
What?	¿Qué?	keh
What is it?	¿Qué es esto?	keh es es-toe
Why?	¿Por qué?	pore keh
Who?	¿Quién?	kee-yen
Where is . . . ?	¿Dónde está . . . ?	dohn-day es-tah
the train station?	la estación del tren?	la es-tah-see-on del train
the subway station?	la estación del Metro?	la es-ta-see-on del meh-tro
the bus stop?	la parada del autobús?	la pah-rah-dah del oh-toe-boos
the post office?	la oficina de correos?	la oh-fee-see-nah day koh-reh-os
the bank?	el banco?	el bahn-koh
the . . . hotel?	el hotel . . . ?	el oh-tel
the store?	la tienda . . . ?	la tee-en-dah
the cashier?	la caja?	la kah-hah
the . . . museum?	el museo . . . ?	el moo-seh-oh
the hospital?	el hospital?	el ohss-pea-tal
the elevator?	el ascensor?	el ah-sen-sore
the bathroom?	el baño?	el bahn-yoh

Here/there	Aquí/allá	ah-key/ah-yah
Open/closed	Abierto/cerrado	ah-be-er-toe/ ser-ah-doe
Left/right	Izquierda/derecha	iss-key-er-dah/ dare-eh-chah
Straight ahead	Derecho	der-eh-choh
Is it near/far?	¿Está cerca/lejos?	es-tah sair-kah/ leh-hoss
I'd like . . . a room	Quisiera . . . un cuarto/una habitación	kee-see-air-ah oon kwahr-toe/ oo-nah ah-bee-tah-see-on
the key	la llave	lah yah-vay
a newspaper	un periódico	oon pear-ee-oh-dee-koh
a stamp	un timbre de correo	oon team-bray day koh-reh-oh
I'd like to buy . . .	Quisiera comprar . . .	kee-see-air-ah kohm-prahr
cigarettes	cigarrillo	ce-gar-reel-oh
matches	cerillos	ser-ee-ohs
a dictionary	un diccionario	oon deek-see-oh-nah-ree-oh
soap	jabón	hah-bone
a map	un mapa	oon mah-pah
a magazine	una revista	oon-ah reh-veess-tah
paper	papel	pah-pel
envelopes	sobres	so-brace
a postcard	una tarjeta postal	oon-ah tar-het-ah post-ahl
How much is it?	¿Cuánto cuesta?	kwahn-toe kwes-tah
It's expensive/ cheap	Está caro/barato	es-tah kah-roh/ bah-rah-toe
A little/a lot	Un poquito/ mucho . . .	oon poh-kee-toe/ moo-choh
More/less	Más/menos	mahss/men-ohss
Enough/too much/too little	Suficiente/de- masiado/muy poco	soo-fee-see-en-tay/ day-mah-see-ah-doe/moo-ee poh-koh
Telephone	Teléfono	tel-ef-oh-no
Telegram	Telegrama	teh-leh-grah-mah
I am ill/sick	Estoy enfermo(a)	es-toy en-fair-moh(ah)
Please call a doctor	Por favor llame un médico	pore fa-vor ya-may oon med-ee-koh
Help!	¡Auxilio! ¡Ayuda!	owk-see-lee-oh/ ah-yoo-dah

| Fire! | ¡Encendio! | en-*sen*-dee-oo |
| Caution!/Look out! | ¡Cuidado! | kwee-*dah*-doh |

On the Road

Highway	Carretera	car-ray-*ter*-ah
Causeway, paved highway	Calzada	cal-*za*-dah
Route	Ruta	*roo*-tah
Road	Camino	cah-*mee*-no
Street	Calle	*cah*-yeh
Avenue	Avenida	ah-ven-*ee*-dah
Broad, tree-lined boulevard	Paseo	pah-*seh*-oh
Waterfront promenade	Malecón	mal-lay-*cone*
Wharf	Embarcadero	em-bar-cah-*day*-ro

In Town

Church	Templo/Iglesia	*tem*-plo/e-*gles*-se-*ah*
Cathedral	Catedral	cah-tay-*dral*
Neighborhood	Barrio	*bar*-re-o
Foreign exchange shop	Casa de cambio	*cas*-sah day *cam*-be-o
City hall	Ayuntamiento	ah-yoon-tah-mee-*en*-toe
Main square	Zócalo	*zo*-cal-o
Traffic circle	Glorieta	glor-e-*ay*-tah
Market	Mercado (Spanish)/	mer-*cah*-doe/
Inn	Posada	pos-*sah*-dah
Group taxi	Colectivo	co-lec-*tee*-vo
Group taxi along fixed route	Pesero	pi-*seh*-ro

Items of Clothing

Embroidered white smock	Huipil	whee-*peel*
Pleated man's shirt worn outside the pants	Guayabera	gwah-ya-*beh*-ra
Leather sandals	Huaraches	wah-*ra*-chays
Shawl	Rebozo	ray-*bozh*-o
Pancho or blanket	Serape	seh-*ra*-peh

Dining Out

A bottle of . . .	Una botella de . . .	*oo*-nah bo-*tay*-yah deh
A cup of . . .	Una taza de . . .	*oo*-nah *tah*-sah deh
A glass of . . .	Un vaso de . . .	oon *vah*-so deh
Ashtray	Un cenicero	oon sen-ee-*seh*-roh
Bill/check	La cuenta	lah *kwen*-tah
Bread	El pan	el pahn
Breakfast	El desayuno	el day-sigh-*oon*-oh
Butter	La mantequilla	lah mahn-tay-*key*-yah
Cheers!	¡Salud!	sah-*lood*
Cocktail	Un aperitivo	oon ah-pair-ee-*tee*-voh
Dinner	La cena	lah *seh*-nah
Dish	Un plato	oon *plah*-toe
Dish of the day	El platillo de hoy	el plah-*tee*-yo day oy
Enjoy!	¡Buen provecho!	bwen pro-*veh*-cho
Fixed-price menu	La comida corrida	lah koh-*me*-dah co-*ree*-dah
Fork	El tenedor	el ten-eh-*door*
Is the tip included?	¿Está incluida la propina?	es-*tah* in-clue-*ee*-dah lah pro-*pea*-nah
Knife	El cuchillo	el koo-*chee*-yo
Lunch	La comida	lah koh-*me*-dah
Menu	La carta	lah *cart*-ah
Napkin	La servilleta	lah sair-vee-*yet*-uh
Pepper	La pimienta	lah pea-me-*en*-tah
Please give me	Por favor déme	pore fah-*vor* *day*-may
Salt	La sal	lah sahl
Spoon	Una cuchara	oo-nah koo-*chah*-rah
Sugar	El azúcar	el ah-*sue*-car
Waiter!/Waitress!	¡Por favor Señor/Señorita!	pore fah-*vor* sen-*yor*/sen-yor-*ee*-tah

INDEX

✕ = *restaurant*, 🏨 = *hotel*

NOTES

NOTES

NOTES

NOTES

NOTES

NOTES

NOTES

NOTES

NOTES

Fodor's Travel Publications

Available at bookstores everywhere, or call 1–800–533–6478, 24 hours a d

Gold Guides

U.S.

Alaska

Arizona

Boston

California

Cape Cod, Martha's Vineyard, Nantucket

The Carolinas & the Georgia Coast

Chicago

Colorado

Florida

Hawai'i

Las Vegas, Reno, Tahoe

Los Angeles

Maine, Vermont, New Hampshire

Maui & Lana'i

Miami & the Keys

New England

New Orleans

New York City

Pacific North Coast

Philadelphia & the Pennsylvania Dutch Country

The Rockies

San Diego

San Francisco

Santa Fe, Taos, Albuquerque

Seattle & Vancouv

The South

U.S. & British Virg Islands

USA

Virginia & Maryla

Washington, D.C.

Foreign

Australia

Austria

The Bahamas

Belize & Guatemala

Bermuda

Canada

Cancún, Cozumel, Yucatán Peninsula

Caribbean

China

Costa Rica

Cuba

The Czech Republic & Slovakia

Eastern & Central Europe

Europe

Florence, Tuscany & Umbria

France

Germany

Great Britain

Greece

Hong Kong

India

Ireland

Israel

Italy

Japan

London

Madrid & Barcelona

Mexico

Montréal & Québec City

Moscow, St. Petersburg, Kiev

The Netherlands, Belgium & Luxembourg

New Zealand

Norway

Nova Scotia, New Brunswick, Prince Edward Island

Paris

Portugal

Provence & the Riviera

Scandinavia

Scotland

Singapore

South Africa

South America

Southeast Asia

Spain

Sweden

Switzerland

Thailand

Tokyo

Toronto

Turkey

Vienna & the Danube

Fodor's Special-Interest Guides

Caribbean Ports of Call

The Complete Guide to America's National Parks

Family Adventures

Fodor's Gay Guide to the USA

Halliday's New England Food Explorer

Halliday's New Orleans Food Explorer

Healthy Escapes

Kodak Guide to Shooting Great Travel Pictures

Net Travel

Nights to Imagine

Rock & Roll Traveler USA

Sunday in New York

Sunday in San Francisco

Walt Disney World for Adults

Walt Disney World, Universal Studios and Orlando

Where Should We Take the Kids? California

Where Should We Take the Kids? Northeast

Worldwide Cruise and Ports of Call

WHEREVER YOU TRAVEL, *H*ELP IS NEVER FAR AWAY.

From planning your trip to providing travel assistance along the way, American Express® Travel Service Offices are always there to help.

Puerto Rico

Travel Network (R)
8 W. Mendez Vigo Street
Mayagüez
787/834-3300

Travel Network (R)
1035 Ashford Ave.
Condado Area
San Juan
787/725-0960

Travel

http://www.americanexpress.com/travel